Scrum and XP from the Trenches

How we do Scrum

Written By:
Henrik Kniberg

© 2007 C4Media Inc
All rights reserved.

C4Media, Publisher of InfoQ.com.

This book is part of the InfoQ Enterprise Software Development series of books.

For information or ordering of this or other InfoQ books, please contact books@c4media.com.

Managing Editor: Diana Plesa

Library of Congress Cataloguing-in-Publication Data:

ISBN: 978-1-4303-2264-1

Printed in the United States of America

Acknowledgements

The first draft of this paper took only one weekend to type, but it sure was an intensive weekend! 150% focus factor :o)

Thanks to my wife Sophia and kids Dave and Jenny for putting up with my asocialness that weekend, and to Sophia's parents Eva and Jörgen for coming over to help take care of the family.

Thanks also to my colleagues at Crisp in Stockholm and people on the scrumdevelopment yahoo group for proofreading and helping me improve the paper.

And, finally, thanks to all my readers who have provided a constant stream of useful feedback. I'm particularly glad to hear that this paper has sparked so many of you to give agile software development a shot!

Contents

Foreword by Jeff Sutherland

Teams need to know Scrum basics. How do you create and estimate a Product Backlog? How do you turn it into a Sprint Backlog? How do you manage a Burndown Chart and calculate your team velocity? Henrik's book is a starter kit of basic   practices that help teams move beyond trying to do Scrum to executing Scrum well.

Good Scrum execution is becoming more important for teams who want investment funding. As an Agile coach for a venture capital group, I help with their goal of investing only in Agile companies that execute Agile practices well. The Senior Partner of the group is asking all portfolio companies if they know the velocity of their teams. They have difficulty answering the question right now. Future investment opportunities will require that development teams understand their velocity of software production.

Why is this so important? If the teams do not know velocity, the Product Owner cannot create a product roadmap with credible release dates. Without dependable release dates, the company could fail and investors could lose their money!

This problem is faced by companies large and small, new or old, funded or not funded. At a recent discussion of Google's   implementation of Scrum at a London conference, I asked an audience of 135 people how many were doing Scrum and 30 responded positively. I then asked them if they were doing   iterative development by Nokia standards. Iterative development is fundamental to the Agile Manifesto – deliver working software early and often. After years of retrospectives with hundreds of Scrum teams, Nokia developed some basic requirements for iterative development:

- Iterations must have fixed time boxes and be less than six weeks long.
- Code at the end of the iteration must be tested by QA and be working properly.

Of the 30 people who said they were doing Scrum, only half said they were meeting the first principle of the Agile Manifesto by Nokia standards. I then asked them if they met the Nokia standards for Scrum:

- A Scrum team must have a Product Owner and know who that person is.
- The Product Owner must have a Product Backlog with estimates created by the team.
- The team must have a Burndown Chart and know their velocity.
- There must be no one outside a team interfering with the team during a Sprint.

Of 30 people doing Scrum, only 3 met the Nokia test for a Scrum team. These are the only teams that will receive future investment by my venture partners.

The value of Henrik's book is that if you follow practices he outlines, you will have a Product Backlog, estimates for the Product Backlog, a Burndown Chart, and know your team velocity along with many other essential practices for a highly functional Scrum. You will meet the Nokia test for Scrum and be worthy of investment in your work. If you are a startup company, you might even receive funding by a venture capital group. You may be the future of software development and creator of the next generation of leading software products.

Jeff Sutherland,
Ph.D., Co-Creator of Scrum

Foreword by Mike Cohn

Both Scrum and Extreme Programming (XP) ask teams to complete some tangible piece of shippable work by the end of each iteration. These iterations are designed to be short and timeboxed. This focus on delivering working code in a short timeframe means that Scrum and XP teams don't have time for theories. They don't pursue drawing the perfect UML model in a case tool, writing the perfect requirements document, or writing code that will be able to accommodate all imaginable future changes. Instead, Scrum and XP teams focus on getting things done. These teams accept that they may mistakes along the way, but they also realize that the best way to find those mistakes is to stop thinking about the software at the theoretical level of analysis and design and to dive in, get their hands dirty, and start building the product.

It is this same focus on doing rather than theorizing that distinguishes this book. That Henrik Kniberg understands this is apparent right from the start. He doesn't offer a lengthy description of what Scrum is; he refers us to some simple websites for that. Instead, Henrik jumps right in and immediately begins describing how his team manages and works with their product backlog. From there he moves through all of the other elements and practices of a well-run agile project. No theorizing. No references. No footnotes. None are needed. Henrik's book isn't a philosophical explanation of why Scrum works or why you might want to try this or that. It is a description of how one well-running agile team works.

This is why the book's subtitle, "How We Do Scrum," is so apt. It may not be the way *you* do Scrum, it's how Henrik's team does Scrum. You may ask why you should care how another team does Scrum. You should care because we can all learn how to do Scrum better by hearing stories of how it has been done by others, especially those who are doing it well. There is not and never will be a list of "Scrum Best Practices" because team and project context trump all other considerations. Instead of best practices, what we need to know are good practices and the contexts in which they were successful. Read enough stories of successful teams and how they did things and you'll be prepared for the obstacles thrown at you in your use of Scrum and XP.

Henrik provides a host of good practices along with the necessary context to help us learn better how to do Scrum and XP in the trenches of our own projects.

Mike Cohn
Author of *Agile Estimating and Planning* **and** *User Stories Applied for Agile Software Development.*

Preface - Hey, Scrum worked!

Scrum worked! For us at least (meaning my current client in Stockholm, who's name I don't intend to mention here). Hope it will work for you too! Maybe this paper will help you along the way.

This is the first time I've seen a development methodology (sorry Ken, a *framework*) work right off the book. Plug 'n play. All of us are happy with it – developers, testers, managers. It helped us get out of a tough situation and has enabled us to maintain focus and momentum despite severe market turbulence and staff reductions.

I shouldn't say I was surprised but, well, I was. After initially digesting a few books on the topic Scrum seemed good, but almost too good to be true (and we all know the saying "when something seems too good to be true..."). So I was justifiably a bit skeptical. But after doing Scrum for a year I'm sufficiently impressed (and most people in my teams as well) that I will probably continue using Scrum by default in new projects whenever there isn't a strong reason not to.

1

Intro

You are about to start using Scrum in your organization. Or perhaps you've been using Scrum for a few months. You've got the basics, you've read the books, maybe you've even taken your Scrum Master certification. Congratulations!

But yet you feel confused.

In Ken Schwaber's words, Scrum is not a methodology, it is a *framework*. What that means is that Scrum is not really going to tell you exactly what to do. Darn.

The good news is I am going to tell you exactly how I do Scrum, in painful excruciating detail. The bad news is, well, that this is only how I do Scrum. That doesn't mean *you* should do it exactly the same way. In fact, I may well do it in a different way if I encounter a different situation.

The strength and pain of Scrum is that you are forced to adapt it to your specific situation.

My current approach to Scrum is the result of one year's Scrum experimentation in a development team of approximately 40 people. The company was in a tough situation with high overtime, severe quality problems, constant firefighting, missed deadlines, etc. The company had decided to use Scrum but not really completed the implementation, which was to be my task. To most people in the development team at that time, "Scrum" was just a strange buzzword they heard echo in the hallway from time to time, with no implication to their daily work.

Over a year's time we implemented Scrum through all layers in the company, tried different team sizes (3 – 12 people), different sprint lengths (2 – 6 weeks), different ways of defining "done", different formats for product backlogs and sprint backlogs (Excel, Jira, index cards), different testing strategies, different ways of doing demos, different ways of synchronizing multiple Scrum teams, etc. We also experimented with XP practices – different ways of doing continuous build, pair programming, test driven development, etc, and how to combine this with Scrum.

This is a constant learning process so the story does not end here. I'm convinced that this company will keep learning (if they keep up the sprint retrospectives) and gain new insights on how to best implement Scrum in their particular context.

Disclaimer

This document does not claim to represent "the right" way to do Scrum! It only represents one way to do Scrum, the result of constant refinement over a year's time. You might even decide that we've got it all wrong.

Everything in this document reflects my own personal subjective opinions and is no means an official statement from Crisp or my current client. For this reason I have intentionally avoided mentioning any specific products or people.

Why I wrote this

When learning about Scrum I read the relevant Scrum and agile books, poured over sites and forums on Scrum, took Ken Schwaber's certification, peppered him with questions, and spent lots of time discussing with my colleagues. One of the most valuable sources of information, however, was actual war stories. The war stories turn Principles and Practices into... well.... How Do You Actually Do It. They also helped me identify (and sometimes avoid) typical Scrum newbie mistakes.

So, this is my chance to give something back. Here's my war story.

I hope that this paper will prompt some useful feedback from those of you in the same situation. Please enlighten me!

But what is Scrum?

Oh, sorry. You are completely new to Scrum or XP? In that case you might want to take a look at the following links:
* http://agilemanifesto.org/
* http://www.mountaingoatsoftware.com/scrum
* http://www.xprogramming.com/xpmag/whatisxp.htm

If you are too impatient to do that, feel free to just read on. Must of the Scrum jargon is explained as we go along so you might still find this interesting.

2

How we do product backlogs

The product backlog is the heart of Scrum. This is where it all starts. The product backlog is basically a prioritized list of requirements, or stories, or features, or whatevers. Things that the customer wants, described using the customer's terminology.

We call these *stories*, or sometimes just *backlog items*.

Our stories include the following fields:

- **ID** – a unique identification, just an auto-incremented number. This is to avoid losing track of stories when we rename them.
- **Name** – a short, descriptive name of the story. For example "See your own transaction history". Clear enough so that developers and the product owner understand approximately what we are talking about, and clear enough to distinguish it from other stories. Normally 2 – 10 words.
- **Importance** – the product owner's importance rating for this story. For example 10. Or 150. High = more important.
  - o I tend to avoid the term "priority" since priority 1 is typically considered the "highest" priority, which gets ugly if you later on decide that something else is even *more* important. What priority rating should *that* get? Priority 0? Priority -1?
- **Initial estimate** – the team's initial assessment of how much work is needed to implement this story compared to other stories. The unit is story points and usually corresponds roughly to "ideal man-days".
  - o Ask the team "if you can take the optimal number of people for this story (not too few and not too many, typically 2), and lock yourselves into a room with lots of food and work completely undisturbed, after how many days will you come out with a finished, demonstratable, tested, releasable implementation?". If the answer is "with 3 guys locked into a room it will take

approximately 4 days" then the initial estimate is 12 story points.

 o The important thing is not to get the absolute estimates correct (i.e. that a 2-point story should take 2 days), the important thing is to get the relative estimates correct (i.e. that a 2-point story should require about half as much work as a 4-point story).

- **How to demo** – a high-level description of how this story will be demonstrated at the sprint demo. This is essentially a simple test spec. "Do this, then do that, then this should happen".

 o If you practice TDD (test-driven development) this description can be used as pseudo-code for your acceptance test code.

- **Notes** – any other info, clarifications, references to other sources of info, etc. Normally very brief.

PRODUCT BACKLOG (example)					
ID	**Name**	**Imp**	**Est**	**How to demo**	**Notes**
1	Deposit	30	5	Log in, open deposit page, deposit €10, go to my balance page and check that it has increased by €10.	Need a UML sequence diagram. No need to worry about encryption for now.
2	See your own transaction history	10	8	Log in, click on "transactions". Do a deposit. Go back to transactions, check that the new deposit shows up.	Use paging to avoid large DB queries. Design similar to view users page.

We experimented with lots of other fields, but at the end of the day, the six fields above were the only ones that we actually used sprint after sprint.

We usually do this in an Excel document with sharing enabled (i.e. multiple users can edit simultaneously). Officially the product owner owns this document, but we don't want to lock other users out. Many times a developer wants to open the document to clarify something or change an estimate.

For the same reason, we don't place this document in the version control repository; we place it on a shared drive instead. This turned out to be the simplest way to allow multiple simultaneous editors without causing lock or merge conflicts.

Almost all other artifacts, however, are placed in the version control repository.

Additional story fields

Sometimes we use additional fields in the product backlog, mostly as a convenience for the product owner to help him sort out his priorities.

- **Track** – a rough categorization of this story, for example "back office" or "optimization". That way the product owner can easily filter out all "optimization" items and set their priority to low, etc.
- **Components** - Usually realized as "checkboxes" in the Excel document, for example "database, server, client". Here the team or product owner can identify which technical components will be involved in implementing this story. This is useful when you have multiple Scrum teams, for example a back office team and a client team, and want to make it easier for each team to decide which stories to take on.
- **Requestor** – the product owner may want to keep track of which customer or stakeholder originally requested the item, in order to give him feedback on the progress.
- **Bug tracking ID** – if you have a separate bug tracking system, like we do with Jira, it is useful to keep track of any direct correspondence between a story and one or more reported bugs.

How we keep the product backlog at a business level

If the product owner has a technical background he might add stories such as "Add indexes to the Events table". Why does he want this? The real underlying goal is probably something like "speed up the search event form in the back office".

It may turn out that indexes weren't the bottleneck causing the form to be slow. It may be something completely different. The team is normally better suited to figure out *how* to solve something, so the product owner should focus on business goals.

When I see technically oriented stories like this, I normally ask the product owner a series of "but *why*" questions until we find the underlying goal. Then we rephrase the story in terms of the underlying goal ("speed up the search event form in the back office"). The original technical description ends up as a note ("Indexing the event table might solve this").

3

How we prepare for sprint planning

OK, sprint planning day is coming at us quickly. One lesson we learn over and over is:

Lesson: Make sure the product backlog is in shipshape *before* the sprint planning meeting.

And what does *that* mean? That all stories have to be perfectly well-defined? That all estimates have to be correct? That all priorities must be fixed? No, no, and no! All it means is:

- The product backlog should exist! (imagine that?)
- There should be *one* product backlog and *one* product owner (per product that is).
- All important items should have importance ratings assigned to them, *different* importance ratings.
    - Actually, it is OK if lower-importance items all have the same value, since they probably won't be brought up during the sprint planning meeting anyway.
    - Any story that the product owner believes has a remote possibility of being included in the next sprint should have a unique importance level.
    - The importance rating is only used to sort the items by importance. So if Item A has importance 20 and Item B has importance 100, that simply means B is more important than A. It does *not* mean that B is five times more important than A. If B had importance rating 21 it will still mean the exact same thing!
    - It is useful to leave gaps in the number sequence in case an item C comes up that is more important than A but less important than B. Of course you could use an importance rating of 20.5 for C, but that gets ugly, so we leave gaps instead!
- The product owner should *understand* each story (normally he is the author, but in some cases other people add requests, which the product owner can prioritize). He does not need to know

exactly what needs to be implemented, but he should understand why the story is there.

Note: Other people than the product owner may add stories to the product backlog. But they may not assign an importance level, that is the product owner's sole right. They may not add time estimates either, that is the team's sole right.

Other approaches that we've tried or evaluated:
- Using Jira (our bug tracking system) to house the product backlog. Most of our product owners find it too click intensive however. Excel is nice and easy to direct-manipulate. You can easily color code, rearrange items, add new columns on an ad-hoc basis, add notes, import and export data, etc
- Using an agile process support tool such as VersionOne, ScrumWorks, XPlanner, etc. We haven't gotten around to testing any of those but we probably will.

4

How we do sprint planning

Sprint planning is a critical meeting, probably the most important event in Scrum (in my subjective opinion of course). A badly executed sprint planning meeting can mess up a whole sprint.

The purpose of the sprint planning meeting is to give the team enough information to be able to work in undisturbed peace for a few weeks, and to give the product owner enough confidence to let them do so.

OK, that was fuzzy. The concrete output of the sprint planning meeting is:
- A sprint goal.
- A list of team members (and their commitment levels, if not 100%).
- A sprint backlog (= a list of stories included in the sprint).
- A defined sprint demo date.
- A defined time and place for the daily scrum.

Why the product owner has to attend

Sometimes product owners are reluctant to spend hours with the team doing sprint planning. "Guys, I've already listed what I want. I don't have time to be at your planning meeting". That is a pretty serious problem.

The reason why the whole team *and* the product owner have to be at the sprint planning meeting is because each story contains three variables that are highly dependent on each other.

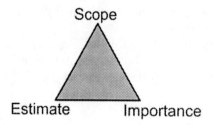

Scope and importance are set by the product owner. Estimate is set by the team. During a sprint planning meeting, these three variables are fine-tuned continuously through face-to-face dialog between the team and the product owner.

Normally the product owner starts the meeting by summarizing his goal for the sprint and the most important stories. Next, the team goes through and time-estimates each story, starting with the most important one. As they do this, they will come up with important scope questions – "does this 'delete user' story include going through each pending transaction for that user and canceling it?'" In some cases the answers will be surprising to the team, prompting them to change their estimates.

In some cases the time estimate for a story won't be what the product owner expected. This may prompt him to change the importance of the story. Or change the scope of the story, which in turn will cause the team to re-estimate, etc, etc.

This type of direct collaboration is fundamental to Scrum and, in fact, all agile software development.

What if the product owner still insists that he doesn't have time to join sprint planning meetings? I usually try one of the following strategies, in the given order:

- Try to help the product owner understand why his direct participation is crucial and hope that he changes his mind.
- Try to get someone in the team to volunteer as product owner proxy during the meeting. Tell the product owner "Since you can't join our meeting, we will let Jeff here represent you as a proxy. He will be fully empowered to change priorities and scope of stories on your behalf during the meeting. I suggest you synchronize with him as much as possible before the meeting. If you don't like Jeff to be proxy please suggest someone else, as long as that person can join us for the full length of the meeting."
- Try to convince the management team to assign a new product owner.
- Postpone the sprint launch until the product owner finds time to join the meeting. In the meantime, refuse to commit to any deliveries. Let the team spend each day doing whatever they feel is most important that day.

Why quality is not negotiable

In the triangle above I intentionally avoided a fourth variable *quality*.

I try to distinguish between *internal quality* and *external quality*.

- *External quality* is what is perceived by the users of the system. A slow and non-intuitive user interface is an example of poor external quality.
- *Internal quality* refers to issues that usually aren't visible to the user, but which have a profound effect on the maintainability of the system. Things like system design consistency, test coverage, code readability, refactoring, etc.

Generally speaking, a system with high internal quality can still have a low external quality. But a system with low internal quality will rarely have a high external quality. It is hard to build something nice on top of a rotten fundament.

I treat external quality as part of scope. In some cases it might make perfect business sense to release a version of the system that has a clumsy and slow user interface, and then release a cleaned up version later. I leave that tradeoff to the product owner, since he is responsible for determining scope.

Internal quality, however, is not up for discussion. It is the team's responsibility to maintain the system's quality under all circumstances and this is simply not negotiable. Ever.

(Well, OK, *almost* never)

So how do we tell the difference between internal quality issues and external quality issues?

Let's say the product owner says "OK guys, I respect your time estimate of 6 story points, but I'm sure you can do some kind of quick-fix for this in half the time if you just put your mind to it."

Aha! He is trying to use internal quality as a variable. How do I know? Because he wants us to reduce the estimate of the story without "paying the price" of reducing the scope. The word "quick-fix" should trigger an alarm in your head...

And why don't we allow this?

My experience is that sacrificing internal quality is almost always a terrible, terrible idea. The time saved is far outweighed by the cost in both short and long term. Once a code base is permitted to start deteriorating it is very hard to put the quality back in later.

Instead I try to steer the discussion towards scope instead. "Since it is important for you to get this feature out early, can we reduce the scope so that it will be quicker to implement? Perhaps we can simplify the error handling and make 'Advanced error handling' a separate story that we save for the future? Or can we reduce the priority of other stories so that we can focus on this one?"

Once the product owner has learned that internal quality isn't negotiable he usually gets quite good at manipulating the other variables instead.

Sprint planning meetings that drag on and on...

The most difficult thing about sprint planning meetings is that:
1) People don't think they will take so long time
2) ... but they do!

Everything in Scrum is time-boxed. I love that one, simple, consistent rule. We try to stick to it.

So what do we do when the time-boxed sprint planning meeting is nearing the end and there is no sign of a sprint goal or sprint backlog? Do we just cut it short??? Or do we extend it for an hour? Or do we end the meeting and continue the next day?

This happens over and over, especially for new teams. So what do you do? I don't know. But what do we do? Oh, um, well, usually I brutally cut the meeting short. End it. Let the sprint suffer. More specifically, I tell the team and product owner "so, this meeting ends in 10 minutes. We don't have much of a sprint plan really. Should we make do with what we have, or should we schedule another 4-hour sprint planning meeting tomorrow from 8 am?". You can guess what they will answer... :o)

I've tried letting the meeting drag on. That usually doesn't accomplish anything, because people are tired. If they haven't produced a decent sprint plan in 2 – 8 hours (or however long your time-box is), they probably won't manage it given another hour. The next option is actually quite OK, to schedule a new meeting next day. Except that people usually are impatient and want to get going with the sprint, and not spend another bunch of hours planning.

So I cut it short. And yes, the sprint suffers. The upside, however, is that the team has learned a very valuable lesson, and the next sprint planning meeting will be much more efficient. In addition, people will be less resistant when you propose a meeting length that they previously would have thought was too long.

Learn to keep to your time-boxes, learn to set realistic time-box lengths. That applies both to meeting lengths and sprint lengths.

Sprint planning meeting agenda

Having some kind of preliminary schedule for the sprint planning meeting will reduce the risk of breaking the timebox.

Here's an example of a typical schedule for us.

Sprint planning meeting: 13:00 – 17:00 (10 minute break each hour)

- **13:00 – 13:30.** Product owner goes through sprint goal and summarizes product backlog. Demo place, date and time is set.
- **13:30 – 15:00.** Team time-estimates, and breaks down items as necessary. Product owner updates importance ratings as necessary. Items are clarified. "How to demo" is filled in for all high-importance items.
- **15:00 – 16:00.** Team selects stories to be included in sprint. Do velocity calculations as a reality check.
- **16:00 – 17:00.** Select time and place for daily scrum (if different from last sprint). Further breakdown of stories into tasks.

The schedule is by no means strictly enforced. The Scrum master may lengthen or shorten the sub-time-boxes as necessary as the meeting progresses.

Defining the sprint length

One of the outputs of the sprint planning meeting is a defined sprint demo date. That means you have to decide on a sprint length.

So what is a good sprint length?

Well, short sprints are good. They allow the company to be "agile", i.e. change direction often. Short sprints = short feedback cycle = more frequent deliveries = more frequent customer feedback = less time spent running in the wrong direction = learn and improve faster, etc.

But then, long sprints are good too. The team gets more time to build up momentum, they get more room to recover from problems and still make the sprint goal, you get less overhead in terms of sprint planning meetings, demos, etc.

Generally speaking product owners like short sprints and developers like long sprints. So sprint length is a compromise. We experimented a lot with this and came up with our favorite length: 3 weeks. Most of our teams (but not all) do 3 week sprints. Short enough to give us adequate corporate agility, long enough for the team to achieve flow and recover from problems that pop up in the sprint.

One thing we have concluded is: *do* experiment with sprint lengths initially. Don't waste too much time *analyzing*, just select a decent length and give it a shot for a sprint or two, then change length.

However, once you have decided what length you like best, *stick to it* for an extended period of time. After a few months of experimentation we found that 3 weeks was good. So we do 3 week sprints, period. Sometimes it will feel slightly too long, sometimes slightly too short. But by keeping the same length this becomes like a corporate heartbeat which everyone comfortably settles into. There is no argument about release dates and such because everyone knows that every 3 weeks there is a release, period.

Defining the sprint goal

It happens almost every time. At some point during the sprint planning meeting I ask "so what is the goal of this sprint?" and everybody just stares blankly back at me and the product owner furrows his brow and itches his chin.

For some reason it is *hard* to come up with a sprint goal. But yet I have found that it really pays to squeeze one out. Better a half-crappy goal than none at all. The goal could be "make more money" or "complete the three top-priority stories" or "impress the CEO" or "make the system good enough to deploy to a live beta group" or "add basic back office support" or whatever. The important thing is that it should be in business terms, not technical terms. This means in terms that people outside the team can understand.

The sprint goal should answer the fundamental question "*Why* are we doing this sprint? Why don't we all just go on vacation instead?". In fact, one way to wheedle a sprint goal out of the product owner is to literally ask that question.

The goal should be something that has not already been achieved. "Impress the CEO" might be a fine goal, but not if he is already impressed by the system as it stands now. In that case everybody could go home and the sprint goal will still be achieved.

The sprint goal may seem rather silly and contrived during the sprint planning, but it often comes to use in mid-sprint, when people are starting to get confused about what they should be doing. If you have several Scrum teams (like we do) working on different products it is very useful to be able to list the sprint goals of all teams on a single wiki page (or whatever) and put them up on a prominent space so that everybody in the company (not only top-level management) knows what the company is doing – and why!

Deciding which stories to include in the sprint

One of the main activities of the sprint planning meeting is to decide which stories to include in the sprint. More specifically, which stories from the product backlog to copy to the sprint backlog.

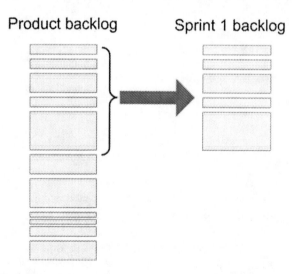

Look at the picture above. Each rectangle represents a story, sorted by importance. The most important story is at the top of the list. The size of each rectangle represents the size of that story (i.e. time estimate in story points). The height of the blue brace represents the team's *estimated*

velocity, i.e. how many story points the team believes they can complete during next sprint.

The sprint backlog to the right is a snapshot of stories from the product backlog. It represents the list of stories that the team will commit to for this sprint.

The *team* decides how many stories to include in the sprint. Not the product owner or anybody else.

This raises two questions:
1. How does the team decide which stories to include in the sprint?
2. How can the product owner affect their decision?

I'll start with the second question.

How can product owner affect which stories make it to the sprint?

Let's say we have the following situation during a sprint planning meeting.

Product backlog

The product owner is disappointed that story D won't be included in the sprint. What are his options during the sprint planning meeting?

One option is to reprioritize. If he gives item D the highest importance level the team will be obliged to add that to the sprint first (in this case bumping out story C).

Option 1

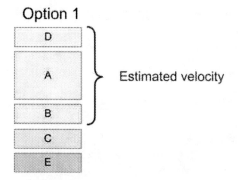

The second option is to change the scope – reduce the scope of story A until the team believes that story D will fit into the sprint.

Option 2

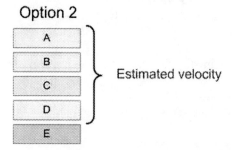

The third option is to split a story. The product owner might decide that there are some aspects of story A that really aren't that important, so he splits A into two stories A1 and A2 with different importance levels.

Option 3

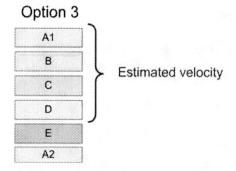

As you see, although the product owner normally can't control the estimated velocity, there are many ways in which he can influence which stories make it into the sprint.

How does the team decide which stories to include in the sprint?

We use two techniques for this:
1. Gut feel
2. Velocity calculations

Estimating using gut feel

- **Scrum master**: "Hey guys, can we finish story A in this sprint?" (points to the most important item in the product backlog)
- **Lisa**: "Duh. Of course we can. We have 3 weeks, and that's a pretty trivial feature."
- **Scrum master**: "OK, what if we add story B as well?" (points to the second most important item)
- **Tom & Lisa in unison**: "Still a no-brainer."
- **Scrum master**: "OK, what about story A and B and C then?"
- **Sam (to product owner)**: "does story C include advanced error handling?"
- **Product owner**: "no, you can skip that for now, just implement basic error handling."
- **Sam**: "then C should be fine as well."
- **Scrum master**: "OK, what if we add story D?"
- **Lisa**: "Hmm...."
- **Tom**: "I think we could do it."
- **Scrum master**: "90% confident? 50%?"
- **Lisa & Tom**: "Pretty much 90%".
- **Scrum master**: "OK, D is in then. What if we add story E?"
- **Sam**: "Maybe."
- **Scrum master**: "90%? 50%?"
- **Sam**: "I'd say closer to 50%".
- **Lisa**: "I'm doubtful."
- **Scrum master**: "OK, then we leave it out. We'll commit to A, B, C, and D. We will of course finish E if we can, but nobody should count on it so we'll leave it out of the sprint plan. How about that?"
- **Everybody**: "OK!"

Gut feel works pretty well for small teams and short sprints.

Estimating using velocity calculations

This technique involves two steps:
1. Decide *estimated velocity*
2. Calculate how many stories you can add without exceeding estimated velocity

Velocity is a measurement of "amount of work done", where each item is weighted in terms of its initial estimate.

The picture below shows an example of *estimated velocity* at the beginning of a sprint and *actual velocity* at the end of that sprint. Each rectangle is a story, and the number inside is the initial estimate of that story.

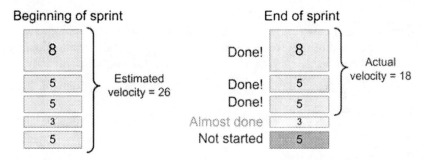

Note that the actual velocity is based on the *initial* estimates of each story. Any updates to the story time estimates done during the sprint are ignored.

I can hear your objection already: "How is this useful? A high or low velocity may depend on a whole bunch of factors! Dimwitted programmers, incorrect initial estimates, scope creep, unplanned disturbances during sprint, etc!"

I agree, it is a crude number. But it is still a useful number, especially when compared to nothing at all. It gives you some hard facts. "Regardless of the reasons, here is the approximate difference between how much we thought we would get done and how much we actually got done".

What about a story that got *almost* completed during a sprint? Why don't we get partial points for that in our actual velocity? Well this is to stress the fact the Scrum (and in fact agile software development and lean manufacturing in general) is all about getting stuff completely, shippably, done! The value of stuff half-done is zero (may in fact be negative). Pick up Donald Reinertsen's "Managing the Design Factory" or one of Poppendieck's books for more on that.

So through what arcane magic do we estimate velocity?

One very simple way to estimate velocity is to look at the team's history. What was their velocity during the past few sprints? Then assume that the velocity will be roughly the same next sprint.

This technique is known as *yesterday's weather*. It is only feasible for teams that have done a few sprints already (so statistics are available) and will do the next sprint in pretty much the same way, with the same team size and same working conditions etc. This is of course not always the case.

A more sophisticated variant is to do a simple resource calculation. Let's say we are planning a 3 week sprint (15 work days) with a 4-person team. Lisa will be on vacation 2 days. Dave is only 50% available and will be on vacation 1 day. Putting all this together...

	AVAILABLE DAYS
TOM	15
LISA	13
SAM	15
DAVE	7
	50 AVAILABLE MAN-DAYS

...gives us 50 available man-days for this sprint.

Is that our estimated velocity? No! Because our unit of estimation is *story points* which, in our case, corresponds roughly to "ideal man-days". An ideal man-day is a perfectly effective, undisturbed day, which is rare. Furthermore, we have to take into account things such as unplanned work being added to the sprint, people being sick, etc.

So our estimated velocity will certainly be less than 50. But how much less? We use the term "focus factor" for this.

THIS SPRINT'S ESTIMATED VELOCITY:

$$(\text{AVAILABLE MAN-DAYS}) \times (\text{FOCUS FACTOR}) = (\text{ESTIMATED VELOCITY})$$

Focus factor is an estimate of how focused the team is. A low focus factor may mean that the team expects to have many disturbances or expects their own time estimates to be optimistic.

The best way to determine a reasonable focus factor is to look at the last sprint (or even better, average the last few sprints).

LAST SPRINT'S FOCUS FACTOR:

$$(\text{FOCUS FACTOR}) = \frac{(\text{ACTUAL VELOCITY})}{(\text{AVAILABLE MAN-DAYS})}$$

Actual velocity is the sum of the initial estimates of all stories that were completed last sprint.

Let's say last sprint completed 18 story points using a 3-person team consisting of Tom, Lisa, and Sam working 3 weeks for a total of 45 man-days. And now we are trying to figure out our estimated velocity for the upcoming sprint. To complicate things, a new guy Dave is joining the team for that sprint. Taking vacations and stuff into account we have 50 man-days next sprint.

So our estimated velocity for the upcoming sprint is 20 story points. That means the team should add stories to the sprint until it adds up to approximately 20.

Beginning of this sprint

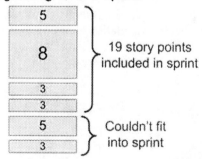

In this case the team may choose the top 4 stories for a total of 19 story points, or the top 5 stories for a total of 24 story points. Let's say they choose 4 stories, since that came closest to 20 story points. When in doubt, choose fewer stories.

Since these 4 stories add up to 19 story points, their final estimated velocity for this sprint is 19.

Yesterday's weather is a handy technique but use it with a dose of common sense. If last sprint was an unusually bad sprint because most of the team was sick for a week, then it may be safe to assume that you won't be that unlucky again and you could estimate a higher focus factor next sprint. If the team has recently installed a new lightning-fast continuous build system you could probably increase focus factor due to that as well. If a new person is joining this sprint you need to decrease focus factor to take his training into account. Etc.

Whenever possible, look back several sprints and average out the numbers to get more reliable estimates.

What if the team is completely new so you don't have any statistics? Look at the focus factor of other teams under similar circumstances.

What if you have no other teams to look at? Guess a focus factor. The good news is that your guess will only apply to the first sprint. After that you will have statistics and can continuously measure and improve your focus factor and estimated velocity.

The "default" focus factor I use for new teams is usually 70%, since that is where most of our other teams have ended up over time.

Which estimating technique do we use?

I mentioned several techniques above - gut feeling, velocity calculation based on yesterday's weather, and velocity calculation based on available man-days and estimated focus factor.

So which technique do we use?

We usually combine all these techniques to a certain degree. Doesn't really take long.

We look at focus factor and actual velocity from last sprint. We look at our total resource availability this sprint and estimate a focus factor. We discuss any differences between these two focus factors and make adjustments as necessary.

Once we have a preliminary list of stories to be included in the sprint I do a "gut feeling" check. I ask the team to ignore the numbers for a moment and just think about if this *feels* like a realistic chunk to bite off for a sprint. If it feels like too much, we remove a story or two. And vice versa.

At the end of the day, the goal is simply to decide which stories to include in the sprint. Focus factor, resource availability, and estimated velocity are just a means to achieve that end.

Why we use index cards

Most of sprint planning meeting is spent dealing with stories in the product backlog. Estimating them, reprioritizing them, clarifying them, breaking them down, etc.

How do we do this in practice?

Well, by default, the teams used to fire up the projector, show the Excel-based backlog, and one guy (typically the product owner or Scrum master) would take the keyboard, mumble through each story and invite discussion. As the team and product owner discussed priorities and details the guy at the keyboard would update the story directly in Excel.

Sounds good? Well it isn't. It usually sucks. And what's worse, the team normally doesn't *notice* that it sucks until they reach the end of the meeting and realize that they still haven't managed to go through the list of stories!

A solution that works much better is to create *index cards* and *put them up on the wall* (or a large table).

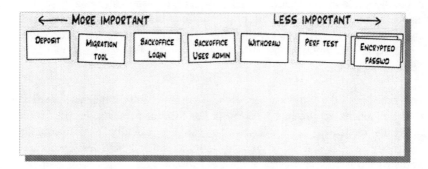

This is a superior user interface compared to computer & projector, because:

- People stand up and walk around => they stay awake and alert longer.
- Everybody feels more personally involved (rather than just the guy with the keyboard).
- Multiple stories can be edited simultaneously.
- Reprioritizing is trivial – just move the index cards around.
- After the meeting, the index cards can be carried right off to the team room and be used as a wall-based taskboard (see pg 45 "How we do sprint backlogs").

You can either write them by hand or (like we usually do) use a simple script to generate printable index cards directly from the product backlog.

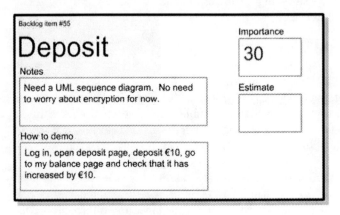

PS – the script is available on my blog at
http://blog.crisp.se/henrikkniberg.

Important: After the sprint planning meeting, our Scrum master manually updates the Excel-based product backlog with respect to any changes that were made to the physical story index cards. Yes, this is a slight administrative hassle but we find this perfectly acceptable considering how much more efficient the sprint planning meeting is with physical index cards.

One note about the "Importance" field. This is the importance as specified in the Excel-based product backlog at the time of printing. Having it on the card makes it easy to sort the cards physically by importance (normally we place more important items to the left, and less important items to the right). However, once the cards are up on the wall you can ignore the importance rating and instead use the physical ordering on the wall to indicate relative importance ratings. If the product owner swaps two items don't waste time updating the importance rating on the paper.

Just make sure you update the importance ratings in the Excel-based product backlog after the meeting.

Time estimates are usually easier to do (and more accurate) if a story is broken down into tasks. Actually we use the term "activity" because the word "task" means something *completely* different in Swedish :o)
This is also nice and easy to do with our index cards. You can have the team divide into pairs and break down one story each, in parallel.

Physically, we do this by adding little post-it notes under each story, each post-it reflecting one task within that story.

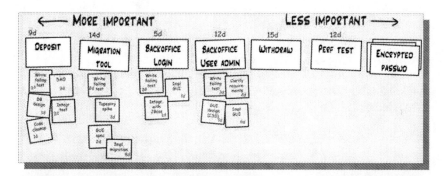

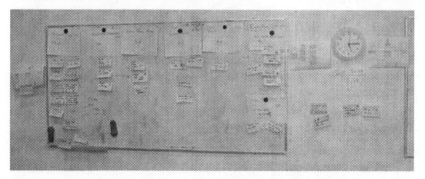

We don't update the Excel-based product backlog with respect to our task breakdowns, for two reasons:

- The task breakdown is usually quite volatile, i.e. they are frequently changed and refined during the sprint, so it is too much of a hassle to keep the product backlog Excel synchronized.
- The product owner doesn't need to be involved at this level of detail anyway.

Just as with the story index cards, the task breakdown post-its can be directly reused in the sprint backlog (see pg 45 "How we do sprint backlogs").

Definition of "done"

It is important that the product owner and the team agree on a clear definition of "done". Is a story complete when all code is checked in? Or is it complete only when it has been deployed to a test environment and verified by an integration test team? Whenever possible we use the done definition "ready to deploy to production" but sometimes we have to make do with the done definition "deployed on test server and ready for acceptance test".

In the beginning we used to have detailed checklists for this. Now we often just say "a story is done when the tester in the Scrum team says so". It is then up to the tester to make sure that product owner's intent is understood by the team, and that the item is "done" enough to pass the accepted definition of done.

We've come to realize that all stories cannot be treated the same. A story named "Query users form" will be treated very differently from a story named "Operations manual". In the latter case, the definition of "done" might simply mean "accepted by the operations team". That is why common sense is often better than formal checklists.

If you often run into confusion about the definition of done (which we did in the beginning) you should probably have a "definition of done" field on each individual story.

Time estimating using planning poker

Estimating is a team activity - every team member is usually involved in estimating every story. Why?

- At the time of planning, we normally don't know exactly who will be implementing which parts of which stories.
- Stories normally involve several people and different types of expertise (user interface design, coding, testing, etc).
- In order to provide an estimate, a team member needs some kind of understanding of what the story is about. By asking everybody to estimate each item, we make sure that each team member understands what each item is about. This increases the likelihood that team members will help each other out during the

sprint. This also increases the likelihood that important questions about the story come up early.

■   When asking everybody to estimate a story we often discover discrepancies where two different team members have wildly different estimates for the same story. That kind of stuff is better to discover and discuss earlier than later.

If you ask the team to provide an estimate, normally the person who understands the story best will be the first one to blurt one out. Unfortunately, this will strongly affect everybody else's estimates.

There is an excellent technique to avoid this – it is called planning poker (coined by Mike Cohn I think).

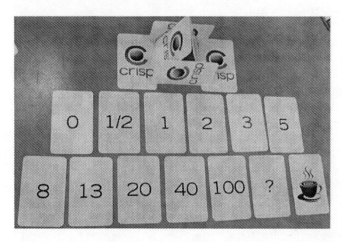

Each team member gets a deck of 13 cards as shown above. Whenever a story is to be estimated, each team member selects a card that represents his time estimate (in story points) and places it face-down on the table. When all team members are done the cards on the table are revealed simultaneously. That way each team member is forced to think for himself rather than lean on somebody else's estimate.

If there is a large discrepancy between two estimates, the team discusses the differences and tries to build a common picture of what work is involved in the story. They might do some kind of task breakdown. Afterwards, the team estimates again. This loop is repeated until the time estimates converge, i.e. all estimates are *approximately* the same for that story.

It is important to remind team members that they are to estimate the total amount of work involved in the story. Not just "their" part of the work. The tester should not just estimate the amount of testing work.

Note that the number sequence is non-linear. For example there is nothing between 40 and 100. Why?

This is to avoid a false sense of accuracy for large time estimates. If a story is estimated at approximately 20 story points, it is not relevant to discuss whether it should be 20 or 18 or 21. All we know is that it is a large story and that it is hard to estimate. So 20 is our ballpark guess.

Want more detailed estimates? Split the story into smaller stories and estimate the smaller stories instead!

And no, you can't cheat by combining a 5 and a 2 to make a 7. You have to choose either 5 or 8, there is no 7.

Some special cards to note:
- 0 = "this story is already done" or "this story is pretty much nothing, just a few minutes of work".
- ? = "I have absolutely no idea at all. None."
- Coffee cup = "I'm too tired to think. Let's take a short break."

Clarifying stories

The worst is when a team proudly demonstrates a new feature at the sprint demo, and the product owner frowns and says "well, that's pretty, but that's *not what I asked for!*"

How do you ensure that the product owner's understanding of a story matches the team's understanding? Or that each team member has the same understanding of each story? Well, you can't. But there are some simple techniques for identifying the most blatant misunderstandings. The simplest technique is simply to make sure that all the fields are filled in for each story (or more specifically, for each story that has high enough importance to be considered for this sprint).

Example 1:
The team and product owner are happy about the sprint plan and ready to end the meeting. The Scrum master says "wait a sec, this story named 'add user', there is no estimate for that. Let's estimate!" After a couple of rounds of planning poker the team agrees on 20 story points whereby the product owner stands up in rage "whaaaat?!". After a few minutes of

heated discussion, it turns out that the team misunderstood the scope 'add user', they thought this meant 'a nice web GUI to add, remove, delete, search users", while the product owner just meant 'add users by manually doing SQL towards DB'. They estimate again and land at 5 story points.

Example 2:
The team and product owner are happy about the sprint plan and ready to end the meeting. The Scrum master says "wait a sec, this story named 'add user', how should that be demonstrated?" Some mumbling ensues and after a minute somebody stands up and says "well, first we log in to the web site, and then..." and the product owner interrupts "log in to the web site?! No, no, no, this functionality should not be part of the web site at all, it should be a silly little SQL script only for tech admins".

The "how to demo" description of a story can (and should) be *very brief!* Otherwise you won't finish the sprint planning meeting on time. It is basically a high level plain-English description of how to execute the most typical test scenario manually. "Do this, then that, then verify this".

I have found that this simple description *often* uncovers important misunderstandings about the scope of a story. Good to discover them early, right?

Breaking down stories into smaller stories

Stories shouldn't be too small or too big (in terms of estimates). If you have a bunch of 0.5-point stories you are probably going to be a victim of micromanagement. On the other hand, a 40-point story stands a high risk of ending up *partially* complete, which produces no value to your company and just increases administration. Furthermore, if your estimated velocity is 70 and your two top-priority stories are weighted 40 story points each, the planning gets kind of difficult. You have to choose between under-committing (i.e. taking just one item) and over-committing (i.e. taking both items).

I find that it is almost always possible to break a large story into smaller stories. Just make sure that the smaller stories still represent deliverables with business value.

We normally strive for stories weighted 2 - 8 man-days. Our velocity is usually around 40-60 for a typical team, so that gives us somewhere around 10 stories per sprint. Sometimes as few as 5 and sometimes as many as 15. That's a manageable number of index cards to deal with.

Breaking down stories into tasks

Wait a sec, what's the difference between "tasks" and "stories"? A very valid question.

The distinction is quite simple. Stories are deliverable stuff that the product owner cares about. Tasks are non-deliverable stuff, or stuff that the product owner doesn't care about.

Example of breaking down a story into smaller stories:

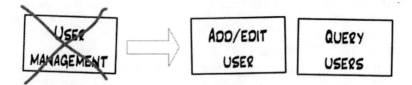

Example of breaking down a story into tasks:

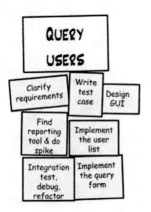

Here are some interesting observations:

- New Scrum teams are reluctant to spending time breaking down a bunch of stories into tasks up-front like this. Some feel this is a waterfall-ish approach.
- For clearly understood stories, it is just as easy to do this breakdown up-front as it is to do later.
- This type of breakdown often reveals additional work that causes the time estimate to go up, and thereby gives a more realistic sprint plan.
- This type of breakdown up-front makes daily scrum meetings noticeably more efficient (see pg 61 "How we do daily scrums").

- Even if the breakdown is inaccurate and will change once work starts, the above advantages still apply.

So, we try to make the sprint planning time-box long enough to fit this in, but if time runs out we let it drop out (see "Where to draw the line" below).

Note – we practice TDD (test driven development) which in effect means that the first task for almost each story is "write a failing test" and the last task is "refactor" (= improve code readability and remove duplication).

Defining time and place for the daily scrum

One frequently-forgotten output of the sprint planning meeting is "a defined time and place for the daily scrum". Without this your sprint will be off to a bad start. The first daily scrum is essentially the kickoff where everybody decides where to start working.

I prefer morning meetings. But, I must admit, we haven't actually tried doing daily scrums in the afternoon or mid-day.

Disadvantage of afternoon scrums: when you come to work in the morning, you have to try to remember what you told people yesterday about what you will be doing today.

Disadvantage of morning scrums: when you come to work in the morning, you have to try to remember what you did yesterday so that you can report this.

My opinion is the first disadvantage is worse, since the most important thing is what you are *going to do*, not what you *did*.

Our default procedure is to select the earliest time at which nobody in the team groans. Usually 9:00, 9:30, or 10:00. The most important thing is that it is a time which everybody in the team can wholeheartedly accept.

Where to draw the line

OK, so time is running out. Of all the stuff we want to do during the sprint planning, what do we cut out if we run out of time?

Well, I use the following priority list:

Priority 1: A sprint goal and demo date. This is the very least you need to start a sprint. The team has a goal, an end date, and they can work right off the product backlog. It sucks, yes, and you should seriously consider scheduling a new sprint planning meeting tomorrow, but if you really need to get the sprint started then this will probably do. To be honest, though, I have never actually started a sprint with this little info.

Priority 2: List of which stories the team has accepted for this sprint.

Priority 3: Estimate filled in for each story in sprint.

Priority 4: "How to demo" filled in for each story in sprint.

Priority 5: Velocity & resource calculations, as a reality check for your sprint plan. Includes list of team members and their commitments (otherwise you can't calculate velocity).

Priority 6: Specified time and place for daily scrum. It only takes a moment to decide, but if you run out of time the Scrum master can simply decide this after the meeting and email everyone.

Priority 7: Stories broken down into tasks. This breakdown can instead be done on a daily basis in conjunction with daily scrums, but will slightly disrupt the flow of the sprint.

Tech stories

Here's a complex issue: Tech stories. Or non-functional items or whatever you want to call them.

I'm referring to stuff that needs to be done but that is not deliverable, not directly related to any specific stories, and not of direct value to the product owner.

We call them "tech stories".

For example:
- **Install continuous build server**
  - o Why it needs to be done: because it saves immense amounts of time for the developers and reduces the risk of big-bang integration problems at the end of an iteration.

- **Write a system design overview**
  - o Why it needs to be done: Because developers keep forgetting the overall design, and thereby write inconsistent code. Need a "the big picture" document to keep everyone on the same page designwise.
- **Refactor the DAO layer**
  - o Why it needs to be done: Because the DAO layer has gotten really messy and is costing everyone time due to confusion and unnecessary bugs. Cleaning the code up will save time for everyone and improve the robustness of the system.
- **Upgrade Jira** (bug tracker)
  - o Why it needs to be done: The current version is too buggy and slow, upgrading will save everyone time.

Are these stories in the normal sense? Or are they tasks that are not connected to any specific story? Who prioritizes these? Should the product owner be involved in this stuff?

We've experimented a lot with different ways of handling tech stories. We tried treating them as first-class stories, just like any others. That was no good, when the product owner prioritized the product backlog it was like comparing apples with oranges. In fact, for obvious reasons, the tech stories were often given low priority with the motivation like "yeah guys, I'm sure a continuous build server is important and all, but let's build some revenue driving features first shall we? Then you can add your tech candy later OK?"

In some cases the product owner is right, but often not. We've concluded that the product owner is not always qualified to be making that tradeoff. So here's what we do:

1) Try to avoid tech stories. Look hard for a way to transform a tech story into a normal story with measurable business value. That way the product owner has a better chance to make correct tradeoffs.
2) If we can't transform a tech story into a normal story, see if the work could be done as a task within another story. For example "refactor the DAO layer" could be a task within the story "edit user", since that involves the DAO layer.
3) If both of the above fail, define it as a tech story, and keep a separate list of such stories. Let the product owner see it but not edit it. Use the "focus factor" and "estimated velocity"

parameters to negotiate with the product owner and bend out some time in the sprint to implement tech stories.

Example (a dialogue very similar to this occurred during one of our sprint planning meetings).

- **Team:** "We have some internal tech stuff that needs to be done. We would like to budget 10% of our time for that, i.e. reduce focus factor from 75% to 65%. Is that OK?"
- **Product owner:** "Hell no! We don't have time!"
- **Team:** "Well, look at the last sprint (all heads turn to the velocity scrawls on the whiteboard). Our estimated velocity was 80, and our actual velocity was 30, right?"
- **PO:** "Exactly! So we don't have time to do internal tech stuff! Need new features!"
- **Team:** "Well, the *reason* why our velocity turned out to be so bad was because we spent so much time trying to put together consistent releases for testing".
- **PO:** "Yes, and?"
- **Team:** "Well, our velocity will probably continue being that bad if we don't do something about it."
- **PO:** "Yes, and?"
- **Team:** "So we propose that we take approximately 10% off of this sprint to set up a continuous build server and other stuff that will take the pain off of integration. This will probably increase our sprint velocity by *at least* 20% for each subsequent sprint, forever!"
- **PO:** "Oh really? Why didn't we do this last sprint then?!"
- **Team:** "Er... because you didn't want us to..."
- **PO:** "Oh, um, well fine, sounds like a good idea to do it now then!"

Of course, the other option is to just keep the product owner out of the loop or give him a non-negotiable focus factor. But there's no excuse not to *try* to reach consensus first.

If the product owner is a competent and reasonable fellow (and we've been lucky there) I suggest keeping him as informed as possible and letting him make the overall priorities. Transparency is one of the core values of Scrum, right?

Bug tracking system vs. product backlog

Here's a tricky issue. Excel is a great format for the product backlog. But you still need a bug tracking system, and Excel will probably not do. We use Jira.

So how do we bring Jira issues into the sprint planning meeting? I mean it wouldn't do to just ignore them and only focus on stories.

We've tried several strategies:
1) Product owner prints out the most high priority Jira items, brings them to the sprint planning meeting, and puts them up on the wall together with the other stories (thereby implicitly specifying the priority of these items compared to the other stories).
2) Product owner creates stories that refer to Jira items. For example "Fix the most critical back office reporting bugs, Jira-124, Jira-126, and Jira-180".
3) Bug-fixing is considered to be outside of the sprint, i.e. the team keeps a low enough focus factor (for example 50%) to ensure that they have time to fix bugs. It is then simply assumed that the team will spend a certain amount of time each sprint fixing Jira-reported bugs
4) Put the product backlog in Jira (i.e. ditch Excel). Treat bugs just like any other story.

We haven't really concluded which strategy is best for us; in fact it varies from team to team and from sprint to sprint. I tend to lean towards the first strategy though. It is nice and simple.

Sprint planning meeting is finally over!

Wow, I never would have thought this chapter on sprint planning meetings would be so long! I guess that reflects my opinion that the sprint planning meeting is the most important thing you do in Scrum. Spend a lot of effort getting that right, and the rest will be so much easier.

The sprint planning meeting is successful if everyone (all team members and the product owner) exit the meeting with a smile, and wake up the next morning with a smile, and do their first daily scrum with a smile.

Then, of course, all kinds of things can go horribly wrong down the line, but at least you can't blame the sprint plan :o)

5

How we communicate sprints

It is important to keep the whole company informed about what is going on. Otherwise people will complain or, even worse, make false assumptions about what is going on.

We use a "sprint info page" for this.

Jackass team, sprint 15

Sprint goal
- Beta-ready release!

Sprint backlog (estimates in parenthesis)
- Deposit (3)
- Migration tool (8)
- Backoffice login (5)
- Backoffice user admin (5)

Estimated velocity: 21

Schedule
- Sprint period: 2006-11-06 to 2006-11-24
- Daily scrum: 9:30 – 9:45, in the team room
- Sprint demo: 2006-11-24, 13:00, in the cafeteria

Team
- Jim
- Erica (scrum master)
- Tom (75%)
- Eva
- John

Sometimes we include info about how each story will be demonstrated as well.

As soon as possible after the sprint planning meeting the Scrum master creates this page, puts it up on the wiki, and sends a spam to the whole company.

```
Subject: Jackass sprint 15 started

Hi all! The Jackass team has now started sprint
15. Our goal is to demonstrate a beta-ready
release on nov 24.

See the sprint info page for details:
http://wiki.mycompany.com/jackass/sprint15
```

We also have a "dashboard" page on our wiki, which links to all currently ongoing sprints.

Corporate Dashboard

Ongoing sprints
- Team X sprint 15
- Team Y sprint 12
- Team Z sprint 1

In addition, the Scrum master prints out the sprint info page and posts on the wall outside his team room. So anybody walking by can look at the sprint info page to find out what that team is doing. Since that includes the time and place for the daily scrum and sprint demo, he knows where to go to find out more.

When the sprint nears the end, the Scrum master reminds everybody about the upcoming demo.

```
Subject: Jackass sprint demo tomorrow at 13:00 in the cafeteria.

Hi all! You are welcome to attend our sprint demo at 13:00 in
the cafeteria tomorrow (friday). We will demonstrate a
beta-ready release.

See the sprint info page for details:
http://wiki.mycompany.com/jackass/sprint15
```

Given all this, nobody really has an excuse *not* to know what's going on.

6

How we do sprint backlogs

You made it this far? Whew, good job.

So now that we've completed the sprint planning meeting and told the world about our shiny new sprint, it is time for the Scrum master to create a sprint backlog. This needs to be done *after* the sprint planning meeting, but *before* the first daily scrum.

Sprint backlog format

We've experimented with different formats for the sprint backlog, including Jira, Excel, and a physical taskboard on the wall. In the beginning we used Excel mostly, there are many publicly available Excel templates for sprint backlogs, including auto generated burn-down charts and stuff like that. I could talk a lot about how we refined our Excel-based sprint backlogs. But I won't. I won't even include an example here.

Instead I'm going to describe in detail what we have found to be the most effective format for the sprint backlog – a wall-based taskboard!

Find a big wall that is unused or contains useless stuff like the company logo, old diagrams or ugly paintings. Clear the wall (ask for permission only if you must). Tape up a big, big sheet of paper (at least 2x2 meters, or 3x2 meters for a large team). Then do this:

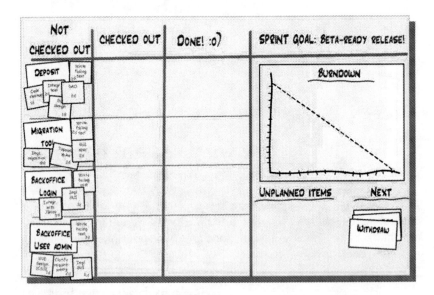

You could of course use a whiteboard. But that's a bit of a waste. If possible, save whiteboards for design scrawls and use non-whiteboard walls for taskboards.

NOTE – if you use post-its for tasks, don't forget to attach them using real tape, or you'll find all the post-its in a neat pile on the floor one day.

How the taskboard works

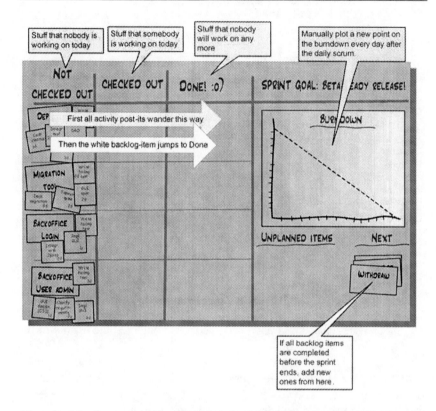

You could of course add all kinds of additional columns. "Waiting for integration test" for example. Or "Cancelled". However before you complicate matters, think deeply. Is this addition really, *really* necessary?

I've found that simplicity is extremely valuable for these types of things, so I only add additional complications when the cost of *not* doing so is too great.

Example 1 – after the first daily scrum

After the first daily scrum, the taskboard might look like this:

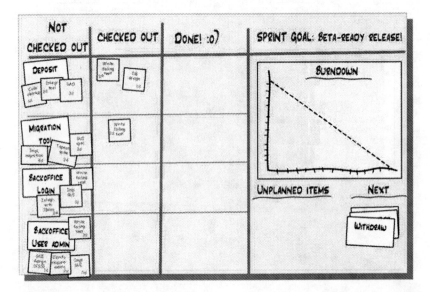

As you can see, three tasks have been "checked out", i.e. the team will be working on these items today.

Sometimes, for larger teams, a task gets stuck in "checked out" because nobody remembers who was working on it. If this happens often in a team they usually introduce policies such labeling each checked out task with the name of the person who checked it out.

Example 2 – after a few more days

A few days later the taskboard might look something like this:

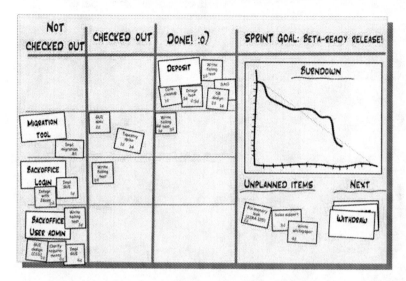

As you can see we've completed the "deposit" story (i.e. it has been checked in to the source code repository, tested, refactored, etc). The migration tool is partially complete, the back office login is started, and the back office user admin is not started.

We've had 3 unplanned items, as you can see down to the right. This is useful to remember when you do the sprint retrospective.

Here's an example of a real sprint backlog near the end of a sprint. It does get rather messy as the sprint progresses, but that's OK since it is short-lived. Every new sprint we create a fresh, clean, new sprint backlog.

How the burndown chart works

Let's zoom in on the burndown chart:

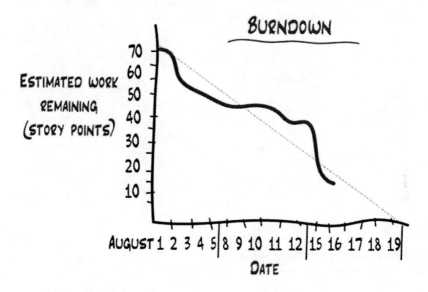

This chart shows that:

- On the first day of the sprint, august 1, the team estimated that there is approximately 70 story points of work left to do. This was in effect the *estimated velocity* of the whole sprint.
- On august 16 the team estimates that there is approximately 15 story points of work left to do. The dashed trend line shows that they are approximately on track, i.e. at this pace they will complete everything by the end of the sprint.

We skip weekends on the x-axis since work is rarely done on weekends. We used to include weekends but this would make the burndown slightly confusing, since it would "flatten out" over weekends which would look like a warning sign.

Taskboard warning signs

A quick glance at the taskboard should give anyone an indication of how well the sprint is progressing. The Scrum master is responsible for making sure that the team acts upon warning signs such as:

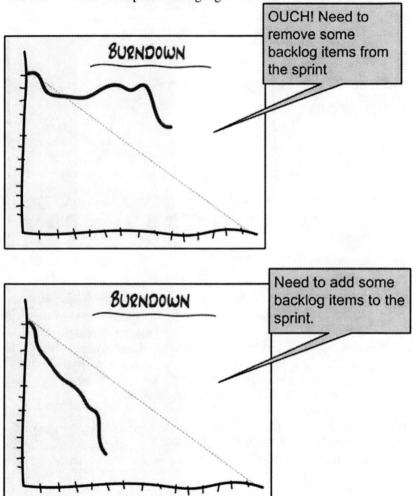

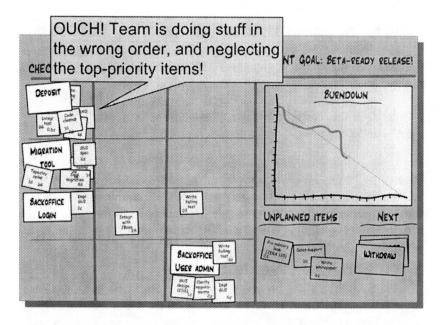

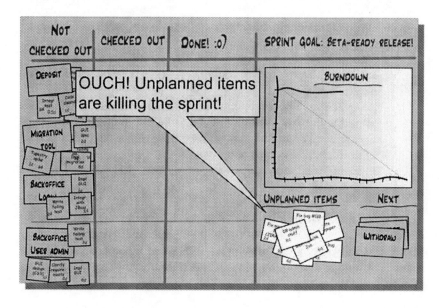

Hey, what about traceability?!

The best traceability I can offer in this model is to take a digital photo of the taskboard every day. If you must. I do that sometimes but never find a need to dig up those photos.

If traceability is very important to you, then perhaps the taskboard solution is not for you.

But I suggest you really try to estimate the actual value of detailed sprint traceability. Once the sprint is done and working code has been delivered and documentation checked in, does anyone really care how many stories were completed at day 5 in the sprint? Does anyone really care what the time estimate for "write a failing test for Deposit" was?

Estimating days vs. hours

In most books and articles on Scrum you'll find that tasks are time-estimated in hours, not days. We used to do that. Our general formula was: 1 effective man-day = 6 effective man-hours.

Now we've stopped doing that, at least in most of our teams, for the following reasons:

- Man-hour estimates were too fine-granular, this tended to encourage too many tiny 1-2 hour tasks and hence micromanagement.
- It turned out that everyone was thinking in terms of man-days anyway, and just multiplying by 6 before writing down man-hours. "Hmmmm, this task should take about a day. Oh I have to write hours, I'll write 6 hours then".
- Two different units cause confusion. "Was that estimate in man-days or man-hours?".

So now we use man-days as a basis for all time estimates (although we call it story points). Our lowest value is 0.5, i.e. any task that is smaller than 0.5 is either removed, combined with some other task, or just left with a 0.5 estimate (no great harm in overestimating slightly). Nice and simple.

7

How we arrange the team room

The design corner

I've noticed that many of the most interesting and valuable design discussions take place spontaneously in front of the taskboard.

For this reason, we try to arrange this area as an explicit "design corner".

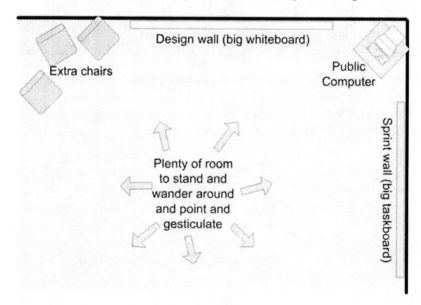

This is really quite useful. There is no better way to get an overview of the system than to stand in the design corner and glance at both walls, then glance at the computer and try the latest build of the system (if you are lucky enough to have continuous build, see pg 81 "How we combine Scrum with XP").

The "design wall" is just a big whiteboard containing the most important design scrawls and printouts of the most important design documentation (sequence charts, GUI prototypes, domain models, etc).

Above: a daily scrum going on in the aforementioned corner.

Hmmmm..... that burndown looks suspiciously nice and straight doesn't it. But the team insists that it is real :o)

Seat the team together!

When it comes to seating and desk layout there is one thing that can't be stressed strongly enough.

Seat the team together!

To clarify that a bit, what I'm saying is

Seat the team together!

People are reluctant to move. At least in the places I've worked. They don't want to have to pick up all their stuff, unplug the computer, move all their junk to a new desk, and plug everything in again. The shorter the distance, the greater the reluctance. "Come ON boss, what's the point of moving just 5 meters?"

When building effective Scrum teams, however, there is no alternative. Just get the team together. Even if you have to personally threaten each individual, carry all their gear, and wipe up their old coffee stains. If there is no space for the team, make space. Somewhere. Even if you have to place the team in the basement. Move tables around, bribe the office manager, do whatever it takes. Just get the team together.

Once you have the team together the payoff will be immediate. After just one sprint the team will agree that it was a good idea to move together (speaking from personal experience that is, there's nothing saying your team won't be too stubborn to admit it).

Now what does "together" mean? How should the desks be laid out? Well, I don't have any strong opinion on the optimal desk layout. And even if I did, I assume most teams don't have the luxury of being able to decide exactly how to layout their desks. There are usually physical constraints – the neighboring team, the toilet door, the big slot machine in the middle of the room, whatever.

"Together" means:
- **Audibility:** Anybody in the team can talk to anybody else without shouting or leaving his desk.
- **Visibility:** Everybody in the team can see everybody else. Everyone can see the taskboard. Not necessarily close enough to be able to *read* it, but at least *see* it.

- **Isolation:** If your whole team were to suddenly stand up and engage in a spontaneous and lively design discussion, there is nobody outside the team close enough to be disturbed. And vice versa.

"Isolation" doesn't mean that the team has to be completely isolated. In a cubicle environment it may be enough that your team has its own cubicle and big enough cubicle walls to filter out *most* of the noise from non-team elements.

And what if you have a distributed team? Well then you are out of luck. Use as many technical aids as you can to minimize the damage – video conferencing, webcams, desktop sharing tools, etc.

Keep the product owner at bay

The product owner should be near enough so that the team can wander over and ask him something, and so that he can wander over to the taskboard. But he should not be seated with the team. Why? Because chances are he will not be able to stop himself from meddling in details, and the team will not "gel" properly (i.e. reach a tight, self-managed, hyperproductive state).

To be honest, this is speculation. I haven't actually seen a case where the product owner is sitting with the team, so I have no actual empirical reason to say that it is a bad idea. Just gut feeling and hearsay from other Scrum masters.

Keep the managers and coaches at bay

This is a bit hard for me to write about, since I was both manager and coach...

It was my job to work as closely with the teams as possible. I set up the teams, moved between them, pair programmed with people, coached Scrum masters, organized sprint planning meetings, etc. In retrospect most people thought this was a Good Thing, since I had some experience with agile software development.

But, then, I was also (enter Darth Vader music) the chief of development, a functional manager role. Which means by entering a team it would automatically become less self-managing. "Heck, boss is here, he probably has lots of opinions on what we should be doing and who should be doing what. I'll let him do the talking."

My point is this; If you are Scrum coach (and perhaps also a manager), do get involved as closely as possible. But only for a limited period, then get out and let the team gel and self-manage. Check up on the team once in a while (not too often) by attending sprint demos and looking at the taskboard and listening in on morning scrums. If you see an improvement area, take the Scrum master aside and coach him. *Not* in front of the team. Another good idea is to attend sprint retrospectives (see pg 67 "How we do sprint retrospectives"), if your team trusts you enough not to let your presence clam them up.

As for well-functioning Scrum teams, make sure they get everything they need, then stay the hell out of the way (except during sprint demos).

8

How we do daily scrums

Our daily scrums are pretty much by the book. They start exactly on time, every day at the same place. In the beginning we would go to a separate room to do sprint planning (those were the days when we used electronic sprint backlogs), however now we do daily scrums in the team room right in front of the taskboard. Nothing can beat that.

We normally do the meetings standing up, since that reduces the risk of surpassing 15 minutes.

How we update the taskboard

We normally update the taskboard during the daily scrum. As each person describes what he did yesterday and will do today, he pulls post-its around on the taskboard. As he describes an unplanned item, he puts up a post-it for that. As he update his time estimates, he writes the new time estimate on the post-it and crosses off the old one. Sometimes the Scrum master does the post-it stuff while people talk.

Some teams have a policy that each person should update the taskboard *before* each meeting. That works fine as well. Just decide on a policy and stick to it.

Regardless of what format your sprint backlog is in, try to get the *whole team* involved in keeping the sprint backlog up-to-date. We've tried doing sprints where the Scrum master is the sole maintainer of the sprint backlog and has to go around every day and ask people about their remaining time estimates. The disadvantages of this are:

- The Scrum master spends too much time administrating stuff, instead of supporting the team and removing impediments.

- Team members are unaware of the status of the sprint, since the sprint backlog is not something they need to care about. This lack of feedback reduces the overall agility and focus of the team.

If the sprint backlog is well-designed it should be just as easy for each team member to update it himself.

Immediately after the daily scrum meeting, someone sums up all the time estimates (ignoring those in the "done" column of course) and plots a new point on the sprint burndown.

Dealing with latecomers

Some teams have a can of coins and bills. When you are late, even if only one minute late, you add a fixed amount to the can. No questions asked. If you call before the meeting and say you'll be late you still have to pay up.

You only get off the hook if you have a good excuse such as a doctor's appointment or your own wedding or something.

The money in the can is used for social events. To buy hamburgers when we have gaming nights for example :o)

This works well. But it is only necessary for teams where people often come late. Some teams don't need this type of scheme.

Dealing with "I don't know what to do today"

It is not uncommon for somebody to say "Yesterday I did bla bla bla, but today I haven't the foggiest clue of what to do" (hey that last bit rhymed). Now what?

Let's say Joe and Lisa are the ones who don't know what to do today.

If I am Scrum master I just move on and let the next guy talk, but make note of which people didn't have anything to do. After everybody's had their say, I go through the taskboard with the whole team, from top to bottom, and check that everything is in sync, that everybody knows what each item means, etc. I invite people to add more post-its. Then I go back to those people who didn't know what to do "now that we've gone through the taskboard, do you have any ideas about what you can do today"? Hopefully they will.

If not, I consider if there is any pair-programming opportunity here. Let's say Niklas is going to implement the back office user admin GUI today. In that case I politely suggest that perhaps Joe or Lisa could pair program with Niklas on that. That usually works.

And if that doesn't work, here's the next trick.

Scrum master: "OK, who wants to demonstrate the beta-ready release to us?" (assuming that was the sprint goal)
Team: confused silence
Scrum master: "Aren't we done?"
Team: "um... no"
Scrum master: "Oh darn. Why not? What's left to do?"
Team: "Well we don't even have a test server to run it on, and the build script is broken."
Scrum master: "Aha." (adds two post-its to the task wall). "Joe and Lisa, how can you help us today?"
Joe: "Um.... I guess I'll try to find some test server somewhere".
Lisa: "... and I'll try to fix that build script".

If you are lucky, someone will actually demonstrate the beta-ready release you asked for. Great! You have achieved your sprint goal. But what if you are in mid-sprint? Easy. Congratulate the team on a job well done, grab one or two of the stories from the "next" section at the bottom right of your taskboard, and move them to the "not checked out" column to the left. Then redo the daily scrum. Notify the product owner that you have added some items to the sprint.

But what if the team has not yet achieved the print goal and Joe and Lisa still refuse to come up with something useful to do. I usually consider one of the following strategies (none of them are very nice, but then this is a last resort):

- **Shame:** "Well if you have no idea how you can help the team, I suggest you go home, or read a book or something. Or just sit around until someone calls for your help.".
- **Old-school:** Simply assign them a task.
- **Peer pressure:** Say "feel free to take your time Joe and Lisa, we'll all just stand here and take it easy until you come up with something to do that will help us reach the goal."
- **Servitude:** Say "Well you can help the team indirectly by being butlers today. Fetch coffee, give people massage, clean up some trash, cook us some lunch, and whatever else we may ask for

during the day." You may be surprised by how fast Joe and Lisa manage to come up with useful technical tasks :o)

If one person frequently forces you to go that far, then you should probably take that person aside and do some serious coaching. If the problem still remains, you need to evaluate whether this person is important to your team or not.

If he *isn't* too important, try to get him removed from your team.

If he *is* important, then try to pair him up with somebody else who can act as his "shepherd". Joe might be a great developer and architect, just that he really prefers other people to tell him what to do. Fine. Give Niklas the duty of being Joe's permanent shepherd. Or take on the duty yourself. If Joe is important enough to your team it will be worth the effort. We've had cases like this and it more or less worked.

9

How we do sprint demos

The sprint demo (or sprint review as some people call it) is an important part of Scrum that people tend to underestimate.

"Oh do we really *have to* do a demo? There really isn't much fun to show!"
"We don't have time to prepare a &%$# demo!"
"I don't have time to attend other team's demos!"

Why we insist that all sprints end with a demo

A well executed sprint demo, although it may seem undramatic, has a profound effect.

- The team gets credit for their accomplishment. They *feel good*.
- Other people learn what your team is doing.
- The demo attracts vital feedback from stakeholders.
- Demos are (or should be) a social event where different teams can interact with each other and discuss their work. This is valuable.
- Doing a demo forces the team to *actually finish stuff* and release it (even if it is only to a test environment). Without demos, we kept getting huge piles of 99% finished stuff. With demos we may get fewer items done, but those items are *really done*, which is (in our case) a lot better than having a whole pile of stuff that is just *sort of done* and will pollute the next sprint.

If a team is more or less forced to do a sprint demo, even when they don't have much that really works, the demo will be embarrassing. The team will stutter and stumble while doing the demo and the applause afterwards will be half-hearted. People will feel a bit sorry for the team, some may be irritated that they wasted time going to a lousy demo.

This hurts. But the effect is like a bitter-tasting medicine. *Next sprint*, the team will really try to get stuff *done*! They will feel that "well, maybe we can only demonstrate 2 things next sprint instead of 5, but dammit this time it's going to WORK!". The team knows that they will have to do a demo no matter what, which significantly increases the chance that there will be something useful to demonstrate. I've seen this happen several times.

Checklist for sprint demos

- Make sure you clearly present the sprint goal. If there are people at the demo who don't know anything about your product, take a few minutes to describe the product.
- Don't spend too much time preparing the demo, especially not on flashy presentations. Cut the crap out and just focus on demonstrating actual working code.
- Keep a high pace, i.e. focus your preparations on making the demo fast-paced rather than beautiful.
- Keep the demo on a business-oriented level, leave out the technical details. Focus on "what did we do" rather than "how did we do it".
- If possible, let the audience try the product for themselves.
- Don't demonstrate a bunch of minor bug fixes and trivial features. Mention them but don't demo them, since that generally takes too long and detracts focus from the more important stories.

Dealing with "undemonstratable" stuff

Team member: "I'm not going to demonstrate this item, because it can't be demonstrated. The story is 'Improve scalability so system can handle 10,000 simultaneous users'. I can't bloody well invite 10,000 simultaneous users to the demo can I?"

Scrum master: "Are you done with the item?"

Team member. "Yes, of course".

Scrum master: "How do you know?"

Team member: "I set the system up in a performance test environment, started 8 load servers and pestered the system with simultaneous requests".

Scrum master: "But do you have any indication that the system will handle 10,000 users".

Team member: "Yes. The test machines are crappy, yet they could handle 50,000 simultaneous requests during my test".

Scrum master: "How do you know?"

Team member (frustrated): "Well I have this report! You can see for yourself, it shows how the test was set up and how many requests were sent!"

Scrum master: "Oh excellent! Then there's your "demo". Just show the report and go through it with the audience. Better than nothing right?".

Team member: "Oh, is that enough? But its ugly, need to polish it up.".

Scrum master: "OK, but don't spend too long. It doesn't have to be pretty, just informative."

10

How we do sprint retrospectives

Why we insist that all teams do retrospectives

The most important thing about retrospectives is to *make sure they happen.*

For some reason, teams don't always seem inclined to do retrospectives. Without gentle prodding most of our teams would often skip the retrospective and move on to the next sprint instead. It may be a cultural thing in Sweden, not sure.

Yet, everybody seems to agree that retrospectives are extremely useful. In fact, I'd say the retrospective is the second most important event in Scrum (the first being the sprint planning meeting) because this is your *best chance to improve!*

Of course, you don't need a retrospective meeting to come up with good ideas, you can do that in your bathtub at home! But will the team accept your idea? Maybe, but the likelihood of getting buy-in from the team is very much higher if the idea comes "from the team", i.e. comes up during the retrospective when everyone is allowed to contribute and discuss the ideas.

Without retrospectives you will find that the team keeps making the same mistakes over and over again.

How we organize retrospectives

The general format varies a bit, but usually we do it something like this:

- We allocate 1 – 3 hours depending on how much discussion is anticipated.
- Participants: The product owner, the whole team, and myself.

- We move off to a closed room, a cozy sofa corner, the rooftop patio, or some place like that. As long as we can have undisturbed discussion.
- We usually don't do retrospectives in the team room, since people's attentions will tend to wander.
- Somebody is designated as secretary.
- The Scrum master shows the sprint backlog and, with help from the team, summarizes the sprint. Important events and decisions, etc.
- We do "the rounds". Each person gets a chance to say, without being interrupted, what they thought was good, what they think could have been better, and what they would like to do differently next sprint.
- We look at the estimated vs. actual velocity. If there is a big difference we try to analyze why.
- When time is almost up the Scrum master tries to summarize concrete suggestions about what we can do better next sprint.

Our retrospectives are generally not too structured. The underlying theme is always the same though: "what can we do better next sprint".

Here is a whiteboard example from a recent retrospective:

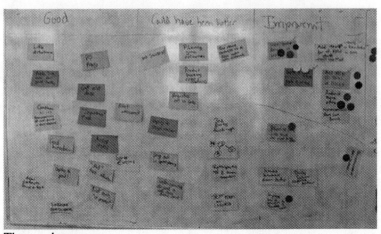

Three columns:
- **Good:** If we could redo the same sprint again, we would do these things the same way.
- **Could have done better:** If we could redo the same sprint again, we would do these things differently.
- **Improvements:** Concrete ideas about how we could improve in the future.

So column 1 and 2 look into the past, while column 3 looks into the future.

After the team brainstormed up all these post-its, they used "dot voting" to determine which improvements to focus on during next sprint. Each team member was given 3 magnets and invited to vote on whatever improvements they would like the team to prioritize during next sprint. Each team member could distribute the magnets as they like, even placing all three on a single issue.

Based on this they selected 5 process improvements to focus on, and will follow this up during next retrospective.

It is important not too get overambitious here. Focus on just a few improvements per sprint.

Spreading lessons learned between teams

The information that comes up during a sprint retrospective is usually extremely valuable. Is this team having a hard time focusing because the sales manager keeps kidnapping programmers to participate as "tech experts" in sales meetings? This is important information. Perhaps other teams are having the same problem? Should we be educating the product management more about our products, so they can do the sales support themselves?

A sprint retrospective is not only about how this one team can do a better job during next sprint, it has wider implications than that.

Our strategy for handling that is very simple. One person (in this case me) attends all sprint retrospectives and acts as the knowledge bridge. Quite informal.

An alternative would be to have each Scrum team publish a sprint retrospective report. We have tried that but found that not many people read such reports, and even fewer act upon them. So we do it the simple way instead.

Important rules for the "knowledge bridge" person:
- He should be a good listener.
- If the retrospective is too silent, he should be prepared to ask simple but well-aimed questions that stimulate discussion within

the group. For example "if you could rewind time and redo this same sprint from day 1, what would you do differently?".

- He should be willing to spend time visiting all retrospectives for all teams.
- He should be in some kind of position of authority, so he can act upon improvement suggestions that are outside the team's control.

This works fairly well but there may be other approaches that work a whole lot better. In that case please enlighten me.

To change or not to change

Let's say the team concludes that "we communicated too little within the team, so we kept stepping on each other's toes and messing up each other's designs."

What should you do about it? Introduce daily design meetings? Introduce new tools to ease communication? Add more wiki pages? Well, maybe. But then again, maybe not.

We've found that, in many cases, just identifying a problem clearly is enough for it to solve itself automatically next sprint. Especially if you post the sprint retrospective on the wall in the team room (which we always forget to do, shame on us!). Every change you introduce has some kind of cost so, before introducing changes, consider doing nothing at all and hoping that the problem will disappear (or become smaller) automatically.

The example above ("we communicated too little within the team...") is a typical example of something that may be best solved by doing nothing at all.

If you introduce a new change every time someone complains about something, people may become reluctant to reveal minor problem areas, which would be terrible.

Examples of things that may come up during retrospectives

Here are some examples of typical things that come up during sprint planning, and typical actions.

"We should have spent more time breaking down stories into sub items and tasks"

This is quite common. Every day at the daily scrum, team members find themselves saying "I don't really know what to do today". So after each daily scrum you spend time finding concrete tasks. Usually more effective to do that upfront.

Typical actions: none. The team will probably sort this out themselves during next sprint planning. If this happens repeatedly, increase the sprint planning time-box.

"Too many external disturbances"

Typical actions:
• ask the team to reduce their focus factor next sprint, so that they have a more realistic plan
• ask the team to record disturbances better next sprint. Who disturbed, how long it took. Will make it easier to solve the problem later.
• ask the team to try to funnel all disturbances to the scrum master or product owner
• ask the team to designate one person as "goalkeeper", all disturbances are routed to him, so that the rest of the team can focus. Could be the Scrum master or a rotating position.

"We overcommitted and only got half of the stuff done"

Typical actions: none. The team will probably not overcommit next sprint. Or at least not overcommit as badly.

"Our office environment is too noisy and messy"

Typical actions:
• try to create a better environment, or move the team offsite. Rent a hotel room. Whatever. See pg 55 "How we arrange the team room').
• If not possible, tell the team to decrease their focus factor next sprint, and to clearly state that this is because of the noisy and messy environment. Hopefully this will cause the product owner to start pestering upper management about this.

Fortunately I've never had to threaten to move the team offsite. But I will if I have to :o)

11

Slack time between sprints

In real life, you can't always sprint. You need to rest between sprints. If you always sprint, you are in effect just jogging.

The same in Scrum and software development in general. Sprints are quite intensive. As a developer you never really get to slack off, every day you have to stand at that danged meeting and tell everyone what you accomplished yesterday. Few will be inclined to say "I spent most of the day with my feet on the table browsing blogs and sipping cappuccino".

In addition to the actual rest itself, there is another good reason to have some slack between sprints. After the sprint demo and retrospective, both the team and the product owner will be full of information and ideas to digest. If they immediately run off and start planning the next sprint, chances are nobody will have had a chance to digest any information or lessons learned, the product owner will not have had time to adjust his priorities after the sprint demo, etc.

Bad:

Monday
09-10: Sprint 1 demo
10-11: Sprint 1 retrospective
13-16: Sprint 2 planning

We try to introduce some kind of slack before starting a new sprint (more specifically, the period *after* the sprint retrospective and *before* the next sprint planning meeting). We don't always succeed though.

At the very least, we try to make sure that the sprint retrospective and the subsequent sprint planning meeting don't occur on the same day. Everybody should at least have a good night's sprintless sleep before starting a new sprint.

Better:

Monday	Tuesday
09-10: Sprint 1 demo 10-11: Sprint 1 retrospective	9-13: Sprint 2 planning

Even better:

Friday	Saturday	Sunday	Monday
09-10: Sprint 1 demo 10-11: Sprint 1 retrospective			9-13: Sprint 2 planning

One way to do this is "lab days" (or whatever you choose to call them). That is, days where developers are allowed to do essentially whatever they want (OK, I admit, inspired by Google). For example read up on the latest tools and APIs, study for a certification, discuss nerdy stuff with colleagues, code a hobby project, etc.

Our goal is to have a lab day between each sprint. That way you get a natural rest between sprints, and you will have a dev team that gets a realistic chance to keep their knowledge up-to-date. Plus it's a pretty attractive employment benefit.

Best?

Thursday	Friday	Saturday	Sunday	Monday
09-10: Sprint 1 demo 10-11: Sprint 1 retrospective	LAB DAY			9-13: Sprint 2 planning

Currently we have lab days once per month. The first Friday every month to be specific. Why not between sprints instead? Well, because I felt it was important that the whole company takes the lab day at the same time. Otherwise people tend to not take it seriously. And since we (so far) don't have aligned sprints across all products, I had to select a sprint-independent lab day interval instead.

We might some day try to synchronize the sprints across all products (i.e. same sprint start and end date for all products and teams). In that case we will definitely place a lab day between each sprint.

12

How we do release planning and fixed price contracts

Sometimes we need to plan ahead more than one sprint at a time. Typically in conjunction with a fixed price contract where we *have* to plan ahead, or else risk signing something that we can't deliver on time.

Typically, release planning for us is an attempt to answer the question *"when,* at *latest,* will we be able to deliver version 1.0 of this new system".

If you *really* want to learn about release planning I suggest you skip this chapter and instead buy Mike Cohn's book "Agile Estimating and Planning". I really wish I had read that book earlier (I read it *after* we had figured this stuff out on our own...). My version of release planning is a bit simplistic but should serve as a good starting point.

Define your acceptance thresholds

In addition to the usual product backlog, the product owner defines a list of *acceptance thresholds* which is a simple classification of what the importance levels in the product backlog actually mean in terms of the contract.

Here's an example of acceptance threshold rules:
- All items with importance >= 100 *must* be included in version 1.0, or else we'll be fined to death.
- All items with importance 50 - 99 *should* be included in version 1.0, but we *might* be able to get away with doing them in a quick follow-up release.
- Items with importance 25 - 49 are required, but can be done in a follow-up release 1.1.
- Items with importance < 25 are speculative and might never be needed at all.

And here's an example of a product backlog, color-coded based on the above rules.

Importance	Name
130	banana
120	apple
115	orange
110	guava
100	pear
95	raisin
80	peanut
70	donut
60	onion
40	grapefruit
35	papaya
10	blueberry
10	peach

Red = must be included in version 1.0 (banana – pear)
Yellow = should be included in version 1.0 (raisin – onion)
Green = may be done later (grapefruit – peach)

So if we deliver everything from banana to onion by the deadline we're safe. If time runs short we *might* get away with skipping raisin, peanut, donut or onion. Everything below onion is bonus.

Time estimate the most important items

In order to do release planning the product owner needs estimates, at least for all stories that are included in the contract. Just like when sprint planning, this is cooperative effort between the product owner and the team – the team estimates, the product owner describes the items and answers questions.

A time estimate is *valuable* if it turns out to be close to correct, less valuable if it turns out to be off by, say, a factor 30%, and completely worthless if it doesn't have any connection to reality.

Here's my take on the value of a time estimate in relation to who calculates it and how long time they spend doing it.

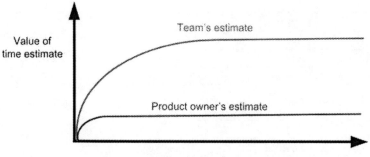

Time spent doing time estimate

All that was just a long-winded way of saying:

- Let the *team* do the estimates.
- Don't make them spend too much time.
- Make sure they understand that the time estimates are *crude estimates*, not *commitments*.

Usually the product owner gathers the whole team in a room, provides some refreshments, and tells them that the goal of this meeting is to time-estimate the top 20 (or whatever) stories in the product backlog. He goes through each story once, and then lets the team get to work. The product owner stays in the room to answer questions and clarify the scope for each item as necessary. Just like when doing sprint planning, the "how to demo" field is a very useful way to lessen the risk of misunderstanding.

This meeting must be strictly time-boxed, otherwise teams tend to spend too much time estimating too few stories.
If the product owner wants more time spent on this he simply schedules another meeting later. The team must make sure that the impact of these meetings on their current sprints is clearly visible to the product owner, so that he understands that their time-estimating work doesn't come for free.

Here is an example of how the time estimates might end up (in story points):

Imp	Name	Estimate
130	banana	12
120	apple	9
115	orange	20
110	guava	8
100	pear	20
95	raisin	12
80	peanut	10
70	donut	8
60	onion	10
40	grapefruit	14
35	papaya	4
10	blueberry	
10	peach	

Estimate velocity

OK, so now we have some kind of crude time estimate for the most important stories.

Next step is to estimate our average velocity per sprint.

This means we need to decide on our focus factor. See pg 24 "How does the team decide which stories to include in the sprint".

Focus factor is basically "how much of the team's time is spent focusing on there currently committed stories". It is never 100% since teams lose time doing unplanned items, doing context switches, helping other teams, checking their email, fixing their broken computer, arguing politics in the kitchen, etc.

Let's say we determine focus factor for the team to be 50% (quite low, we normally hover around 70%). And let's say our sprint length will be 3 weeks (15 days) long and our team size is 6.

Each sprint is thus 90 man-days long, but can only be expected to produce complete 45 man-days worth of stories (due to the 50% focus factor).

So our estimated velocity is 45 story points.

If each story had a time estimate of 5 days (which they don't) then this team would crank out approximately 9 stories per sprint.

Put it together into a release plan

Now that we have time estimates and a velocity (45) we can easily chop the product backlog into sprints:

Imp	Name	Estimate
	Sprint 1	
130	banana	12
120	apple	9
115	orange	20
	Sprint 2	
110	guava	8
100	pear	20
95	raisin	12
	Sprint 3	
80	peanut	10
70	donut	8
60	onion	10
40	grapefruit	14
	Sprint 4	
35	papaya	4
10	blueberry	
10	peach	

Each sprint includes as many stories as possible without exceeding the estimated velocity of 45.

Now we can see that we'll probably need 3 sprints to finish all the "must haves" and "should haves".

3 sprints = 9 calendar weeks = 2 calendar months. Now is that the deadline we promise the customer? Depends entirely on the nature of the contract; how fixed the scope is etc. We usually add a significant buffer to protect against bad time estimates, unexpected problems, unexpected features, etc. So in this case we might agree to set the delivery date to 3 months in the future, giving us 1 month "reserve".

The nice thing is that we can demonstrate something usable to the customer every 3 weeks and invite him to change the requirements as we go along (depending of course on how the contract looks).

Adapting the release plan

Reality will not adapt itself to a plan, so it must be the other way around.

After each sprint we look at the actual velocity for that sprint. If the actual velocity was very different from the estimated velocity, we revise the estimated velocity for future sprints and update the release plan. If this puts us into trouble, the product owner may start negotiating with the customer or start checking how he can reduce scope without breaking the contract. Or perhaps he and the team comes up with some way to increase velocity or increase focus factor by removing some serious impediment that was identified during the sprint.

The product owner might call the customer and say "hi, we're running a bit behind schedule but I believe we can make the deadline if we just remove the "embedded Pacman" feature that takes a lot of time to build. We can add it in the follow-up release 3 weeks after the first release if you like".

Not good news to the customer perhaps, but at least we are being honest and giving the customer an early choice – should we deliver the most important stuff on time or deliver everything late. Usually not a hard choice :o)

13

How we combine Scrum with XP

To say that Scrum and XP (eXtreme Programming) can be fruitfully combined is not really a controversial statement. Most of the stuff I see on the net supports that hypothesis, so I won't spend time arguing why.

Well, I will mention one thing. Scrum focuses on management and organization practices while XP focuses mostly on actual programming practices. That's why they work well together – they address different areas and complement each other.

I hereby add my voice to the existing empirical evidence that Scrum and XP can be fruitfully combined!

I'm going to highlight some of the more valuable XP practices and how they apply to our day-to-day work. Not all our teams have managed to adopt all practices, but in total we've experimented with most aspects of the XP/Scrum combination. Some XP practices are directly addressed by Scrum and can be seen as overlapping, for example "Whole Team", "Sit Together", "Stories", and "Planning game". In those cases we've simply stuck to Scrum.

Pair programming

We started doing this lately in one of our teams. Works quite well actually. Most of our other teams still don't pair program very much but, having actually tried it in one team for a few sprints now, I'm inspired to try to coach more teams into giving it a shot.

Some conclusions so far about pair programming:
- Pair programming does improve code quality.
- Pair programming does improve team focus (for example when the guy behind you says "hey is that stuff really necessary for this sprint?").

- Surprisingly many developers that are strongly against pair programming actually haven't tried it, and quickly learn to like it once they do try it.
- Pair programming is exhaustive and should not be done all day.
- Shifting pairs frequently is good.
- Pair programming does improve knowledge spread within the group. Surprisingly fast too.
- Some people just aren't comfortable with pair programming. Don't throw out an excellent programmer just because he isn't comfortable with pair programming.
- Code review is an OK alternative to pair programming.
- The "navigator" (the guy not using the keyboard) should have a computer of his own as well. Not for development, but for doing little spikes when necessary, browsing documentation when the "driver" (the guy at the keyboard) gets stuck, etc.
- Don't force pair programming upon people. Encourage people and provide the right tools but let them experiment with it at their own pace.

Test-driven development (TDD)

Amen! This, to me, is more important than both Scrum and XP. You can take my house and my TV and my dog, but don't try to stop me from doing TDD! If you don't like TDD then don't let me in the building, because I will try to sneak it in one way or another :o)

Here's a 10 second summary of TDD:

> *Test-driven development means that you write an automated test, then you write just enough code to make that one test pass, then you refactor the code primarily to improve readability and remove duplication. Rinse and repeat.*

Some reflections on test-driven development.
- TDD is *hard*. It takes a while for a programmer to *get it*. In fact, in many cases it doesn't really matter how much you teach and coach and demonstrate – in many cases the only way for a programmer to *get it* is to have him pair program with somebody else who is good at TDD. Once a programmer does *get it*, however, he will usually be severely infected and will never want to work in any other way.
- TDD has a profoundly positive effect on system design.

- It takes time to get TDD up and running effectively in a new product, especially black-box integration tests, but the return on investment is *fast*.
- Make sure you invest the time necessary to make it *easy* to write tests. This means getting the right tools, educating people, providing the right utility classes or base classes, etc.

We use the following tools for test-driven development:

- jUnit / httpUnit / jWebUnit. We are considering TestNG and Selenium.
- HSQLDB as an embedded in-memory DB for testing purposes.
- Jetty as an embedded in-memory web container for testing purposes.
- Cobertura for test coverage metrics.
- Spring framework for wiring up different types of test fixtures (with mocks, without mocks, with external database, with in-memory database, etc).

In our most sophisticated products (from a TDD perspective) we have automated black-box acceptance tests. These tests start up the whole system in memory, including databases and webservers, and access the system using only its public interfaces (for example HTTP).

This makes for extremely fast develop-build-test cycles. This also acts as a safety net, giving the developers confidence enough to refactor often, which means the design stays clean and simple even as the system grows.

TDD on new code

We do TDD for all new development, even if that means initial project setup takes longer (since we need more tools and support for test harnesses etc). That's a bit of a no-brainer, the benefits are so great that there really is no excuse *not* to do TDD.

TDD on old code

TDD is hard, but trying to do TDD on a code base that wasn't built using TDD from start... that's *really hard*! Why? Well, actually, I could write many pages on this topic so I think I'll stop here. I'll save that for my next paper "TDD from the Trenches" :o)

We spent quite a lot of time trying to automate integration testing in one of our more complex systems, a code base that had been around for a while and was in a severely messed up state and completely devoid of tests.

For every release of the system we had a team of dedicated testers who would perform a whole bunch of complex regression and performance tests. The regression tests were mostly manual work. This significantly slowed down our development and release cycle. Our goal was to automate these tests. After banging our heads against the wall for a few months, however, we hadn't really gotten that much closer.

After that we switched approach. We conceded to the fact that we were stuck with manual regression testing, and instead starting asking ourselves "How can we make the manual testing process less time consuming?" This was a gaming system, and we realized that a lot of the test team's time was spent doing quite trivial setup tasks, such as browsing around in the back office to set up tournaments for testing purposes, or waiting around for a scheduled tournament to start. So we created utilities for that. Small, easily accessible shortcuts and scripts that did all the grunt work and let the testers focus on the actual testing.

That effort really paid off! In fact, that is probably what we should have done from start. We were too eager to automate the testing that we forgot to do it step-by-step, where the first step was to build stuff that makes *manual* testing more efficient.

Lesson learned: If you are stuck with having to do manual regression testing, and want to automate this away, don't (unless it is really easy). Instead, build stuff that makes manual regression testing easier. *Then* consider automating the actual testing.

Incremental design

This means keeping the design simple from start and continuously improving it, rather than trying to get it all right from the start and then freezing it.

We're doing fairly well at this, i.e. we spend a reasonable amount of time refactoring and improving existing design, and we rarely spend time doing big up-front designs. Sometimes we screw up of course, for example by allowing a shaky design to "dig in" too strongly so that refactoring becomes a big project. But all in all we're fairly satisfied.

Continuous design improvement is mostly an automatic side effect of doing TDD

Continuous integration

Most of our products have a fairly sophisticated continuous integration setup based on Maven and QuickBuild. This is extremely valuable and time-saving. It is the ultimate solution to the good ol' "hey but it works on *my* machine" issue. Our continuous build server acts as the "judge" or reference point from which to determine the health of all our codebases. Every time someone checks something in to the version control system the continuous build server will wake up, build everything from scratch on a shared server, and run all the tests. If anything goes wrong it will send an email notifying the entire team that the build failed, including info about exactly which code change broke the build, link to test reports, etc.

Every night the continuous build server will rebuild the product from scratch and publish binaries (ears, wars, etc), documentation, test reports, test coverage reports, dependency reports, etc, to our internal documentation portal. Some products will also be automatically deployed to a test environment.

Setting this up was *a lot of work*, but worth every minute.

Collective code ownership

We encourage collective code ownership but not all teams have adopted this yet. We've found that pair programming with frequent rotation of pairs automatically leads to a high level of collective code ownership. Teams with a high level of collective code ownership have proven to be very robust, for example their sprint doesn't die just because some key person is sick.

Informative workspace

All teams have access to whiteboards and empty wall space and make quite good use of this. In most rooms you'll find the walls plastered with all kinds of information about the product and project. The biggest problem is old junk accumulating on the walls, we might introduce a "housekeeper" role in each team.

We encourage the use of taskboards, but not all teams have adopted this yet. See pg 55 "How we arrange the team room."

Coding standard

Lately we've started defining a coding standard. Very useful, wish we had done it earlier. It takes almost no time at all, just start simple and let it grow. Only write down stuff that isn't obvious to everyone and link to existing material whenever possible.

Most programmers have their own distinct coding style. Little details like how they handle exceptions, how they comment code, when they return null, etc. In some cases the difference doesn't matter, in other cases it can lead to a severely inconsistent system design and hard-to-read code. A code standard is very useful here, as long as you focus on the stuff that matters.

Here are some examples from our code standard:

- You may break any of these rules, but make sure there is a good reason and document it.
- Use the Sun code conventions by default: http://java.sun.com/docs/codeconv/html/CodeConvTOC.doc.html
- Never, ever, ever catch exceptions without logging the stack trace or rethrowing. log.debug() is fine, just don't lose that stack trace.
- Use setter-based dependency injection to decouple classes from each other (except of course when tight coupling is desirable).
- Avoid abbreviations. Well-known abbreviations such as DAO are fine.
- Methods that return Collections or arrays should not return null. Return empty collections and arrays instead of null.

Sustainable pace / energized work

Many books on agile software development claim that extended overtime is counterproductive in software development.

After some unwilling experimentation on this I can only agree wholeheartedly!

About a year ago one of our teams (the biggest team) was working insane amounts of overtime. The quality of the existing code base was dismal and they had to spend most of their time firefighting. The test team (which was also doing overtime) didn't have a chance to do any serious quality assurance. Our users were angry and the tabloids were eating us alive.

After a few months we had managed to lower people's work hours to decent levels. People worked normal hours (except during project crunches sometimes). And, surprise, productivity and quality improved noticeably.

Of course, reducing the work hours was by no means the *only* aspect that led to the improvement, but we're all convinced it had a large part in it.

14

How we do testing

This is the hardest part. I'm not sure if it's the hardest part of Scrum, or just the hardest part of software development in general.

Testing is the part that probably will vary most between different organizations. Depending on how many testers you have, how much test automization you have, what type of system you have (just server+webapp? or do you actually ship boxed software?), size of release cycles, how critical the software is (blog server vs. flight control system), etc.

We've experimented quite a lot with how to do testing in Scrum. I'll try to describe what we've been doing and what we've learnt so far.

You probably can't get rid of the acceptance test phase

In the ideal Scrum world, a sprint results in a potentially deployable version of your system. So just deploy it, right?

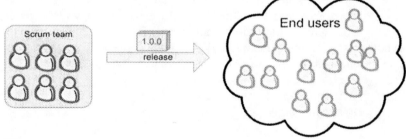

Wrong.

Our experience is that this usually doesn't work. There will be nasty bugs. If quality has any sort of value to you, some kind of manual acceptance testing phase is required. That's when dedicated testers that are *not* part of the team hammer the system with those types of tests that the Scrum team couldn't think of, or didn't have time to do, or didn't have the hardware to do. The testers access the system in exactly the same way as the end users, which means they must be done manually (assuming your system is for human users).

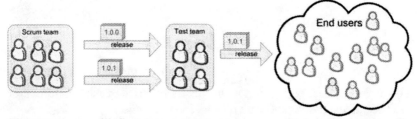

The test team will find bugs, the Scrum team will have to do bug-fix releases, and sooner or later (hopefully sooner) you will be able to release a bug-fixed version 1.0.1 to the end users, rather than the shaky version 1.0.0.

When I say "acceptance test phase" I am referring to the whole period of testing, debugging, and re-releasing until there is a version good enough for production release.

Minimize the acceptance test phase

The acceptance test phase hurts. It feels distinctly un-agile. Although we can't get rid of it, we can (and do) try to minimize it. More specifically, minimize the amount of *time* needed for the acceptance test phase. This is done by:

- Maximizing the quality of the code delivered from the Scrum team
- Maximizing the efficiency of the manual test work (i.e. find the best testers, give them the best tools, make sure they report time-wasting tasks that could be automated)

So how do we maximize the quality of the code delivered from the Scrum team? Well, there are lots of ways. Here are two that we find work very well:

- Put testers in the Scrum team
- Do less per sprint

Increase quality by putting testers in the Scrum team

Yes, I hear both objections:

- "But that's obvious! Scrum teams are supposed to be *cross functional!*"
- "Scrum teams are supposed to be role-less! We can't have a guy who is *only* a tester!"

Let me clarify. What I mean by "tester" in this case is "A guy whose primary skill is testing", rather than "a guy whose role is to do only testing".

Developers are often quite lousy testers. *Especially* developers testing their own code.

The tester is the "signoff guy"

In addition to being "just" a team member, the tester has an important job. He is the signoff guy. Nothing is considered "done" in a sprint until *he* says it's done. I've found that developers often say something is done when it really isn't. Even if you have a very clear definition of "done" (which you really should, see pg 32 "Definition of "done""), developers will frequently forget it. We programmers are impatient people and want to move on to the next item ASAP.

So how does Mr. T (our tester) know something is done then? Well, first of all, he should (surprise) *test* it! In many cases it turns out that something a developer considered to be "done" wasn't even *possible to test!* Because it wasn't checked in, or wasn't deployed to the test server, or couldn't be started, or whatever. Once Mr. T has tested the feature, he should go through the "done" checklist (if you have one) with the developer. For example if the definition of "done" mandates that there should be a release note, then Mr. T checks that there is a release note. If there is some kind of more formal specification for this feature (rare in our case) then Mr. T checks up on that as well. Etc.

A nice side effect of this is that the team now has a guy who is perfectly suited to organize the sprint demo.

What does the tester do when there is nothing to test?

This question keeps coming up. Mr. T: "Hey Scrum master, there's nothing to test at the moment, so what should *I* do?". It may take a week before the team completes the first story, so what should the tester do during *that* time?

Well, first of all, he should be *preparing for tests*. That is, writing test specs, preparing a test environment, etc. So when a developer has something that is ready to test, there should be no waiting, Mr. T should dive right in and start testing.

If the team is doing TDD then people spend time writing test code from day 1. The tester should pair-program with developers that are writing test code. If the tester can't program at all he should still pair-program with developers, except that he should only navigate and let the developer do the typing. A good tester usually comes up with different types of tests than a good developer does, so they complement each other.

If the team is not doing TDD, or if there isn't enough test-case writing to fill up the tester's time, he should simply do whatever he can to help the team achieve the sprint goal. Just like any other team member. If the tester can program then that's great. If not, your team will have to identify all non-programming tasks that need to be done in the sprint.

When breaking down stories into tasks during the sprint planning meeting, the team tends to focus on *programming tasks*. However usually there are lots of *non-programming* tasks that need to be done in the sprint. If you spend time trying to *identify the non-programming tasks* during the sprint planning phase, chances are Mr. T will be able to contribute quite a lot, even if he can't program and there is no testing to do right now.

Examples of non-programming tasks that often need to be done in a sprint:
- Set up a test environment.
- Clarify requirements.
- Discuss deployment details with operations.
- Write deployment documents (release notes, RFC, or whatever your organization does).
- Contact with external resources (GUI designers for example).
- Improve build scripts.
- Further breakdown of stories into tasks.
- Identify key questions from the developers and get them answered.

On the converse side, what do we do if Mr. T becomes a bottleneck? Let's say we are on the last day of the sprint and suddenly lots of stuff is done and Mr. T doesn't have a chance to test everything. What do we do? Well we could make everybody in the team into Mr. T's assistants. He decides which stuff he needs to do himself, and delegates grunt testing to the rest of the team. That's what cross functional teams are all about!

So yes, Mr. T *does* have a special role in the team, but he is still allowed to do other work, and other team members are still allowed to do his work.

Increase quality by doing less per sprint

This goes back to the sprint planning meeting. Simply put, don't cram too many stories items into the sprint! If you have quality problems, or long acceptance test cycles, do less per sprint! This will almost automatically lead to higher quality, shorter acceptance test cycles, fewer bugs affecting end users, and higher productivity in the long run since the team can focus on new stuff all the time rather than fixing old stuff that keeps breaking.

It is almost always cheaper to build less, but build it stable, rather than to build lots of stuff and then have to do panic hot-fixes.

Should acceptance testing be part of the sprint?

We waver a lot here. Some of our teams include acceptance testing in the sprint. Most of our teams however don't, for two reasons:
- A sprint is time-boxed. Acceptance testing (using my definition which includes debugging and re-releasing) is very difficult to time-box. What if time runs out and you still have a critical bug? Are you going to release to production with a critical bug? Are you going to wait until next sprint? In most cases both solutions are unacceptable. So we leave manual acceptance testing outside.
- If you have multiple Scrum teams working on the same product, the manual acceptance testing must be done on the combined result of both team's work. If both teams did manual acceptance within the sprint, you would still need a team to test the final release, which is the integrated build of both team's work.

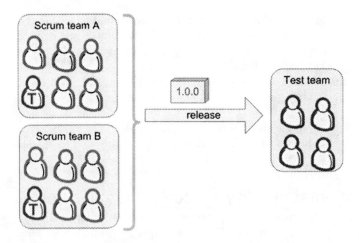

This is by no means a perfect solution but good enough for us in most cases.

Sprint cycles vs. acceptance test cycles

In a perfect McScrum world you don't need acceptance test phases since each Scrum team releases a new production-ready version of your system after each sprint.

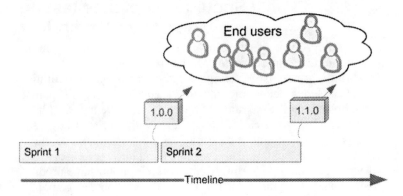

Well, here's a more realistic picture:

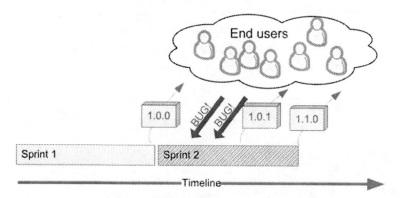

After sprint 1, a buggy version 1.0.0 is released. During sprint 2, bug reports start pouring in and the team spends most of its time debugging and is forced to do a mid-sprint bug-fix release 1.0.1. Then at the end of sprint 2 they release a new feature-version 1.1.0, which of course is even buggier since they had even less time to get it right this time due to all the disturbances from last release. Etc etc.

The diagonal red lines in sprint 2 symbolize chaos.

Not too pretty eh? Well, the sad thing is that the problem remains even if you have an acceptance test team. The only difference is that most of the bug reports will come from the test team instead of from angry end users. That's a huge difference from a business perspective, but for developers it amounts to almost the same thing. Except that testers are usually less aggressive than end users. Usually.

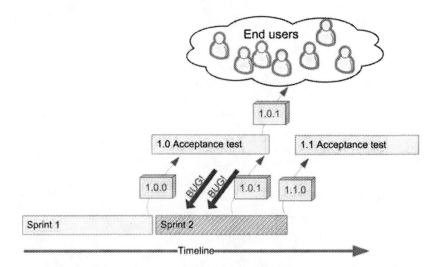

We haven't found any simple solution to this problem. We've experimented a lot with different models though.

First of all, again, maximize the quality of the code that the Scrum team releases. The cost of finding and fixing bugs early, within a sprint, is just so extremely low compared to the cost of finding and fixing bugs afterwards.

But the fact remains, even if we can minimize the number of bugs, there will still be bug reports coming after a sprint is complete. How do we deal with that?

Approach 1: "Don't start building new stuff until the old stuff is in production"

Sounds nice doesn't it? Did you also get that warm fuzzy feeling?

We've been close to adopting this approach several times, and drawn fancy models of how we would do this. However we always changed our minds when we realized the downside. We would have to add a non time-boxed release period between sprints, where we do only testing and debugging until we can make a production release.

We didn't like the notion of having non time-boxed release periods between sprints, mainly because it would break the regular sprint heartbeat. We could no longer say that "every 3 weeks we start a new sprint". Besides, this doesn't completely solve the problem. Even if we have a release period, there will be urgent bug reports coming in from time to time, and we have to be prepared to deal with them.

Approach 2: "OK to start building new stuff, but prioritize getting the old stuff into production"

This is our preferred approach. Right now at least.

Basically, when we finish a sprint we move on to the next one. But we expect to be spending some time in the next sprint fixing bugs from the last sprint. If the next sprint gets severely damaged because we had to spend so much time fixing bugs from the previous sprint, we evaluate why this happened and how we can improve quality. We make sure sprints are long enough to survive a fair amount of bug fixing from the previous sprint.

Gradually, over a period of many months, the amount of time spent fixing bugs from previous sprints decreased. In addition we were able to get fewer people involved when bugs did happen, so that the *whole* team didn't need to get disturbed each time. Now we are at a more acceptable level.

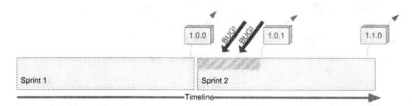

During sprint planning meetings we set the focus factor low enough to account for the time we expect to spend fixing bugs from last sprint. With time, the teams have gotten quite good at estimating this. The velocity metric helps a lot (see pg. 24 "How does the team decide which stories to include in the sprint?").

Bad approach – "focus on building new stuff"

This in effect means "focus on building new stuff *rather than getting old stuff into production*". Who would want to do that? Yet we made this mistake quite often in the beginning, and I'm sure many other companies do as well. It's a stress-related sickness. Many managers don't really understand that, when all the coding is finished, you are usually still far from production release. At least for complex systems. So the manager (or product owner) asks the team to continue adding new stuff while the backpack of old almost-ready-to-release code gets heavier and heavier, slowing everything down.

Don't outrun the slowest link in your chain

Let's say acceptance test is your slowest link. You have too few testers, or the acceptance test period takes long because of the dismal code quality.

Let's say your acceptance test team can test at most 3 features per week (no, we don't use "features per week" as a metric; I'm using it just for this example). And let's say your developers can develop 6 new features per week.

It will be tempting for the managers or product owners (or maybe even the team) to schedule development of 6 new features per week.

Don't! Reality will catch up to you one way or another, and it will hurt.

Instead, schedule 3 new features per week and spend the rest of the time alleviating the testing bottleneck. For example:

- Have a few developers work as testers instead (oh they will love you for that...).
- Implement tools and scripts that make testing easier.
- Add more automated test code.
- Increase sprint length and have acceptance test included in sprint.
- Define some sprints as "test sprints" where the whole team works as an acceptance test team.
- Hire more testers (even if that means removing developers)

We've tried all of these solutions (except the last one). The best long term solution is of course point 2 and 3, i.e. better tools and scripts and test automation.

Retrospectives are a good forum for identifying the slowest link in the chain.

Back to reality

I've probably given you the impression that we have testers in all Scrum teams, that we have a huge acceptance test teams for each product that we release after each sprint, etc, etc.

Well, we don't.

We've *sometimes* managed to do this stuff, and we've seen the positive effects of it. But we are still far from an acceptable quality assurance process, and we still have a lot to learn there.

15

How we handle multiple Scrum teams

A lot of things get much harder when you have multiple Scrum teams working on the same product. That problem is universal and doesn't really have anything to do with Scrum. More developers = more complications.

We have (as usual) experimented with this. At most we had a team of approximately 40 people working on the same product.

The key questions are:
- How many teams to create
- How to allocate people into teams

How many teams to create

If dealing with multiple Scrum teams is so hard, why do we bother? Why not just put everyone in the same team?

The biggest single Scrum team we've had was around 11 people. It worked, but not too well. Daily scrums tended to drag on past 15 minutes. Team members didn't know what other team members were doing, so there would be confusion. It was difficult for the Scrum master to keep everyone aligned towards the goal, and difficult to find time to address all obstacles that were reported.

The alternative is to split into two teams. But is that better? Not necessarily.

If the team is experienced and comfortable with Scrum, and there is a logical way of splitting the roadmap into two distinct tracks, and those two tracks don't both involve the same source code, then I'd say it's a good idea to split the team. Otherwise I'd consider sticking to one team, despite the disadvantage of big teams.

My experience is that it is better to have fewer teams that are too big than to have many small teams that keep interfering with each other. Make small teams only when they don't need to interfere with each other!

Virtual teams

How do you know if you made the right or wrong decision with respect to the "big team" vs. "many teams" tradeoff?

If you keep your eyes and ears open you may notice that "virtual teams" form.

Example 1: You choose to have one large team. But when you start looking at who talks to whom during the sprint, you notice that the team has effectively split into two sub-teams.

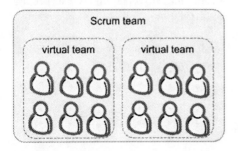

Example 2: You choose to have three smaller teams. But when you start looking at who talks to whom during the sprint, you notice that team 1 and team 2 are talking to each other all the time, while team 3 is working in isolation.

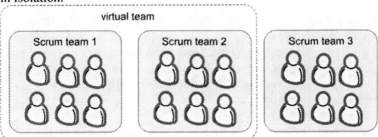

So what does that mean? That your team division strategy was wrong? Yes, if the virtual teams seem to be sort of permanent. No, if the virtual teams seem to be temporary.

Look at example 1 again. If the two virtual sub-teams tend to change once in a while (i.e. people move between the virtual sub-teams) then you probably made the right decision to have them as a single Scrum team. If the two virtual sub-teams stay the same throughout the whole sprint, you probably want to break them apart into two real Scrum teams next sprint.

Now look at example 2 again. If team 1 and team 2 are talking to each (and not team 3) throughout the whole sprint, you probably want to combine team 1 and team 2 into a single Scrum team next sprint. If team 1 and team 2 are talking to each other a lot throughout the first half of the sprint, and then team 1 and team 3 talk to each other throughout the second half of the sprint, then you should consider combining all three teams into one, or just leaving them as three teams. Bring up the question during the sprint retrospective and let the teams decide for themselves.

Team division is one of the really hard parts of Scrum. Don't think too deeply or optimize too hard. Experiment, keep watch for virtual teams, and make sure you take plenty of time to discuss this type of stuff during your retrospectives. Sooner or later you will find the right solution for your particular situation. The important thing is that the teams are comfortable and don't stumble over each other too often.

Optimal team size

Most books I've read claim that the "optimal" team size is somewhere around 5 – 9 people.

From what I've seen so far I can only agree. Although I'd say 3 – 8 people. In fact, I believe it is worth taking some pains to achieve teams of that size.

Let's say you have a single Scrum team of 10 people. Consider ejecting the two weakest team members. Oops, did I just say that?

Let's say you have two different products, with one 3-person team per product, and both are moving too slow. It *might* be a good idea to combine them into one single 6-person team responsible for both products. In that case let one of the two product owners go (or give him an advisory role or something).

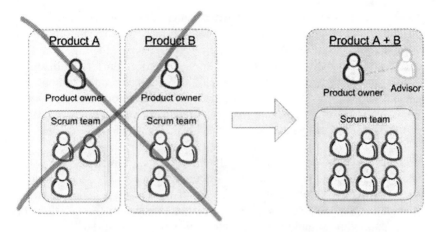

Let's say you have a single 12-person Scrum team, because the code base is in such a crappy state that there is no way for 2 different teams to work on it independently. Put some serious effort into fixing the code base (instead of building new features) until you get to a point where you can split the team. This investment will probably pay off quite quickly.

Synchronized sprints – or not?

Let's say you have three Scrum teams working on the same product. Should their sprints be synchronized, i.e. start and end together? Or should they overlap?

Our first approach was to have overlapping sprints (with respect to time).

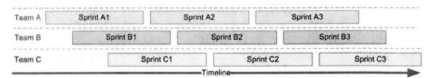

This sounded nice. At any given moment in time there would be an ongoing sprint just about to end and a new sprint just about to begin. The product owner's workload would be evenly spread out over time. There would be releases flowing continuously out of the system. Demos every week. Hallelujah.

Yeah, I know, but it really *did* sound convincing at the time!

We had just started doing this when I one day had the opportunity to talk to Ken Schwaber (in conjunction with my Scrum certification). He pointed out that this was a *bad* idea, that it would be much better to synchronize the sprints. I don't remember his exact reasons, but after some discussion I was convinced.

Team A	Sprint 1	Sprint 2	Sprint 3
Team B	Sprint 1	Sprint 2	Sprint 3
Team C	Sprint 1	Sprint 2	Sprint 3

Timeline ➤

This is the solution we've used ever since, and never regretted it. I'll never know if the overlapping sprints strategy would have failed, but I think so. The advantage of synchronized sprints is:

- There is a natural time at which to rearrange teams – between sprints! With overlapping sprints, there is no way to rearrange teams without disturbing at least one team in mid-sprint.
- All teams could work towards the same goal in a sprint and do sprint planning meetings together, which leads to better collaboration between teams.
- Less administrative overhead, i.e. fewer sprint planning meetings, sprint demos, and releases.

Why we introduced a "team lead" role

Let's say we have a single product with three teams.

The red guy labeled P is Product Owner. The black guys labeled S are Scrum Masters. The rest are ~~grunts~~... er... respectable team members.

With this constellation, who decides which people should be in which teams? The product owner? The three Scrum masters together? Or does every person get to select his own team? But then what if everyone wants to be in team 1 (because Scrum master 1 is so *good looking*)?

What if it later turns out that it is really not possible to have more than two teams working in parallel on this code base, so we need to transform this into two 9-person teams instead of three 6-person teams. That means 2 Scrum masters. So which one of the current 3 Scrum masters will be relieved of his title?

In many companies these will be quite sensitive issues.

It is tempting to let the product owner do the allocation and reassignment of people. But that isn't really product owner stuff right? The product owner is the domain expert who tells the team in which direction they should run. He should not really have to get involved in the nitty gritty details. Especially since he is a "chicken" (if you've heard the chicken and pig metaphor, otherwise google up "chickens and pigs").

We've solved this by introducing a "team lead" role. This corresponds to what you might call "Scrum of Scrums master" or "the boss" or "main Scrum master" etc. He doesn't have to lead any single team, but he is responsible for cross-team issues such as who should be Scrum master for teams, how people should be divided into teams, etc.

We had a hard time coming up with a good name for this role. "Team lead" was the least lousy name we could find.

This solution has worked well for us and I can recommend it (regardless of what you decide to call the role).

How we allocate people to teams

There are two general strategies for allocating people to teams, when you have multiple teams on the same product.
- Let a designated person do the allocation, for example the "team lead" that I mentioned above, the product owner, or the functional manager (if he is involved enough to be able to make good decisions here).
- Let the teams do it themselves somehow.

We've experimented with all three. Three? Yeah. Strategy 1, Strategy 2, and a combination of both.

We found that the combination of both works best.

Before the sprint planning meeting, the team lead calls for a team allocation meeting together with the product owner and all Scrum masters. We talk about last sprint and decide if any team reallocations are warranted. Perhaps we want to combine two teams, or move some people from one team to another. We decide on something and write it down as a *proposed team allocation*, which we bring to the sprint planning meeting.

The first thing we do during the sprint planning meeting is go through the top-priority items in the product backlog. The team lead then say something like:

"Hi everyone. We suggest the following team allocation for next sprint."

Preliminary team allocation		
Team 1 - tom - jerry - donald - mickey	Team 2 - goofy - daffy - humpty - dumpty	Team 3 - minnie - scrooge - winnie - roo

"As you see, this would mean a reduction from 4 to 3 teams. We have listed members for each team. Please group up and grab yourself a wall section."

(team lead waits while people wander around in the room, after a while there are 3 groups of people, each standing next to an empty wall section).

"Now this team division is *preliminary*! It is just a starting point, to save time. As the sprint planning meeting progresses you are free to wander off to another team instead, split your team into two, combine with another team, or whatever. Use common sense based on the product owner's priorities."

This is what we have found works best. A certain level of centralized control initially, followed by a certain level of decentralized optimization afterwards.

Specialized teams – or not?

Let's say your technology consists of three main components:

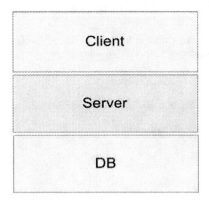

And let's say you have 15 people working on this product, so you really don't want to run them as a single Scrum team. What teams do you create?

Approach 1: component-specialized teams

One approach is to create component-specialized teams such as a "client team", a "server team", and a "DB team".

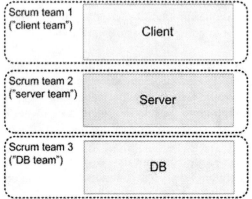

This is where we started. Doesn't work too well, at least not when most stories involve multiple components.

For example let's say we have a story named "notice-board where users can post messages to each other". This notice board feature would involve updating the user interface in the client, adding logic to the server, and adding some tables in the database.

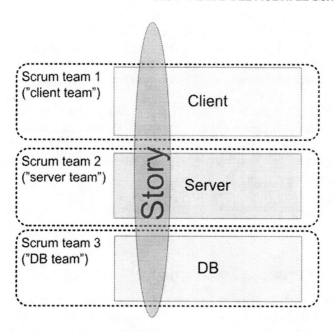

This means all three teams - the client team, the server team, and the DB team - have to collaborate to get this story done. Not too good.

Approach 2: cross-component teams

A second approach is to create cross-component teams, i.e. teams that are not tied to any specific component.

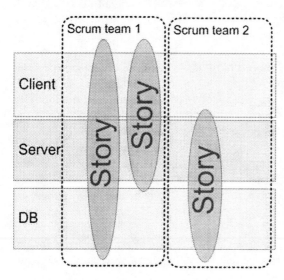

If many of your stories involve multiple components this team type division strategy will work better. Each team can implement a whole story including the client parts, server parts, and DB parts. The teams can thereby work more independently of each other, which is a Good Thing.

One of the first things we did when introducing Scrum was to break up the existing component-specialized teams (approach 1) and create cross-component teams instead (approach 2). This lessened the number of cases of "we can't complete this item because we are waiting for the server guys to do their part."

We do, however, sometimes assemble temporary component-specialized teams when there is a strong need.

Rearrange teams between sprints - or not?

Each sprint is usually quite different from the other, depending on which types of stories that are top priority at that particular moment. As a result, the optimal team setup may be different for each sprint.

In fact, almost every sprint we found ourselves saying something like "*this* sprint isn't really a *normal* sprint because (bla bla bla)....". After a while we just gave up the notion of "normal" sprints. There are no normal sprints. Just like there are no "normal" families or "normal" people.

One sprint it may be a good idea to have a client-only team, consisting of everyone who knows the client code base well. Next sprint it may be a good idea to have two cross-component teams and split the client people between them.

One of the key aspects of Scrum is "team gel", i.e. if a team gets to work together over multiple sprints they will usually become *very tight*. They will learn to achieve *group flow* and reach an incredible productivity level. But it takes a few sprints to get there. If you keep changing the teams around you will never achieve really strong team gel.

So if you do want to rearrange the teams, make sure you consider the consequences. Is this a long term change or a short term change? If it is a short term change considering skipping it. If it is a long term change, go for it.

One exception is when you start doing Scrum with a large team for the first time. In this case it is probably worth experimenting a bit with team subdivision until you find something that everyone is comfortable with. Make sure everybody understands that it is OK to get it all wrong the first few times, as long as you keep improving.

Part-time team members

I can only confirm what the Scrum books say – having part-time members of a Scrum team is generally not a good idea.

Let's say you are about to take on Joe as a part-time member of your Scrum team. Think carefully first. Do you really need Joe on your team? Are you sure you can't get Joe full-time? What are his other commitments? Can someone else take over Joe's other commitment and let Joe taken on a more passive, supportive role with respect to that commitment? Can Joe join your team full time from *next* sprint, and in the mean time transfer his other responsibilities to someone else?

Sometimes there is just no way out. You desperately need Joe because he is the only DBA in the building, but the others teams need him just as badly so he will never be allocated fulltime to your team, and the company can't hire more DBAs. Fine. That's a valid case for having him on a part-time basis (which by the way is exactly what happened to us). But make sure you really do this evaluation every time.

In general I'd rather have a team of 3 full-timers than 8 part-timers.

If you have one person that will divide his time among multiple teams, like the aforementioned DBA, it is a good idea to still have him primarily assigned to one team. Figure out which team is likely to need him the most, and make that his "home team". When nobody else is dragging him off, he will attend that team's daily scrums, sprint planning meetings, retrospectives, etc.

How we do Scrum-of-Scrums

Scrum-of-scrums is basically a regular meeting where all Scrum masters gather up to talk.

At one point in time we had four products, where three of the products only had one Scrum team each, and the last product had 25 people divided into several Scrum teams. Something like this:

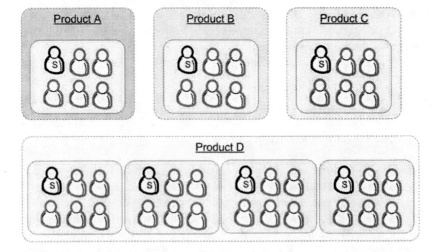

This means we had two levels of Scrum-of-Scrums. We had one "product level" Scrum-of-Scrums consisting of all teams within Product D, and one "corporate level" Scrum-of-Scrums consisting of all products.

Product level Scrum-of-Scrums

This meeting was very important. We did it once per week, sometimes more often than that. We discussed integration issues, team balancing issues, preparations for next sprint planning meeting, etc. We allocated 30 minutes but frequently overran. An alternative would have been to have Scrum-of-Scrums every day but we never got around to trying that.

Our Scrum-of-Scrums agenda was
1) Round the table, everyone describes what their team accomplished last week, what they plan to accomplish this week, and what impediments they have.
2) Any other cross-team concerns that need to be brought up, for example integration issues.

The agenda for Scrum-of-Scrums is not really important to me, the important thing is that you *have* regular Scrum-of-Scrums meetings.

Corporate level Scrum-of-Scrums

We called this meeting "The Pulse". We've done this meeting in a variety of formats, with a variety of participants. Lately we've ditched the whole concept and replaced it with a weekly all-hands (well, all people involved in development) meeting instead. 15 minutes.

What? 15 minutes? All-hands? All members of all teams of all products? Does that work?

Yes it works if you (or whoever runs the meeting) are strict about keeping it short.

The meeting format is:
1) News and updates from the chief of development. Info about upcoming events for example.
2) Round-robin. One person from each product group reports on what they accomplished last week, what they plan to accomplish this week, and any problems. Some other people report as well (CM lead, QA lead, etc).
3) Anybody else is free to add any info or ask questions

This is a forum for brief information, not discussion or reflection. By leaving it at that, 15 minutes usually works. Sometimes we overrun, but very rarely to more than 30 minutes total. If interesting discussions pop up I pause them and invite those who are interested to stay after the meeting and continue the discussion.

Why do we do an all-hands pulse meeting? Because we noticed that the corporate-level Scrum of Scrums was mostly about reporting. We rarely had actual discussions in that group. In addition, many other people outside the group were hungry for this type of info. Basically, teams want to know what others teams are doing. So we figured that if we are going to meet and spend time informing each other about what each team is doing, why not just let everyone attend.

Interleaving the daily scrums

If you have many Scrum teams within a single product, and they all do the daily scrum at the same time, you have a problem. The product owner (and nosy people like me) can only attend one team's daily scrum per day.

So we ask teams to avoid having daily scrums at the same time.

	Room 1	Room 2
9:00	Team 1	
9:15		Team 2
9:30	Team 3	
9:45		Team4
10:00	Team 5	

The sample schedule above is from the period when we had daily scrums in separate rooms, rather than in the team room. The meetings are normally 15 minutes but each team gets a 30-minute slot in the room in case they need to overrun slightly.

This is *extremely useful* for two reasons.

1. People like the product owner and myself can visit *all* daily scrums on a single morning. There's no better way to get an accurate picture of how the sprint is coming along, and what the key threats are.
2. Teams can visit each other's daily scrums. Doesn't happen too often, but once in a while two teams will be working on a similar area, so a few members drop in on each other's daily scrums to stay in sync.

The downside is less freedom for the team – they can't choose any time they like for the daily scrum. This hasn't really been a problem for us though.

Firefighting teams

We had a situation where a large product was unable to adopt Scrum because they spent too much time firefighting, i.e. panic-fixing bugs on their prematurely released system. This was a real vicious cycle, they were so busy firefighting that they didn't have time to work proactively to *prevent* fires (i.e. improve the design, automating tests, create monitoring tools, alarm tools, etc).

We addressed this problem by creating a designated firefighting team, and a designated Scrum team.

The Scrum team's job was to (with the product owner's blessing) try to stabilize the system and, effectively, prevent fires.
The firefighting team (we called them "support" actually) had two jobs.
1) Fight fires
2) Protect the Scrum team from all kinds of disturbances, including things such as fending off ad-hoc feature requests coming in from nowhere.

The firefighting team was placed nearest the door; the Scrum team was placed in the back of the room. So the firefighting team could actually *physically protect* the Scrum team from disturbances such as eager salespeople or angry customers.

Senior developers were placed on both teams, so that one team wouldn't be too dependent on core competence from the other.

This was basically an attempt to solve a Scrum bootstrapping problem. How can we start doing Scrum if the team doesn't have a chance to plan their work more than one day at a time? Our strategy was, as mentioned, to split the group.

This worked pretty well. Since the Scrum team was given room to work proactively they were finally able to stabilize the system. In the meantime the firefighting team completely gave up the notion of being able to plan ahead, they worked completely reactively, just fixing whatever panic issue would come up next.

Of course, the Scrum team was not *completely* undisturbed. Frequently the firefighting team had to involve key people from the Scrum team, or at worst the whole team.

Anyway, after a couple of months the system was stable enough that we could ditch the firefighting team and create additional Scrum teams instead. The firefighters were quite happy to park their battered helmets and join Scrum teams instead.

Splitting the product backlog – or not?

Let's say you have one product and two Scrum teams. How many product backlogs should you have? How many product owners? We've evaluated three models for this. The choice has a pretty big effect on how sprint planning meetings are carried out.

Strategy 1: One product owner, one backlog

This is the "There Can Only Be One" model. Our preferred model.

The good thing about this model is that you can let teams pretty much form themselves based on the product owner's current top priorities. The product owner can focus on *what he needs*, and let the teams decide how to split the work up.

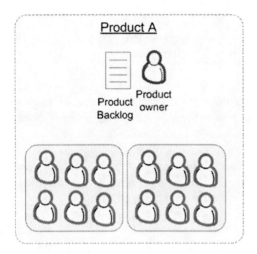

To be more concrete, here's how the sprint planning meeting works for this team:

The sprint planning meeting takes place at an external conference center.

Just before the meeting, the product owner declares one wall to be the "product backlog wall" and puts up stories up there (index cards), ordered by relative priority. He keeps putting them up until that wall is full, which is usually more than enough items for a sprint.

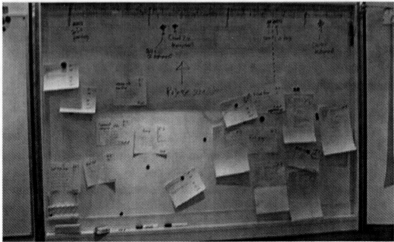

Each Scrum team selects an empty wall section for themselves and posts their team name there. That's their "team wall". Each team then grab stories from the product backlog wall, starting from the top priority stories, and pulls the index cards to their own team wall.

This is illustrated in the picture below, with yellow arrows symbolizing the flow of story index cards from the product backlog wall to the team walls.

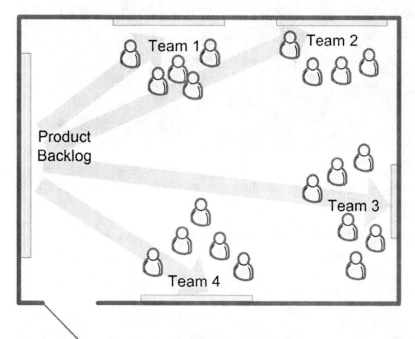

As the meeting progresses, the product owner and the teams haggle over the index cards, moving them around between teams, moving them up and down to change priority, breaking them down into smaller items, etc. After an hour or so, each team has a first candidate version of a sprint backlog on their team wall. After that the teams work independently, time estimating and breaking down to tasks.

It's messy and chaotic and exhausting, but also effective and fun and social. When time is up, all teams usually have enough information to start their sprint.

Strategy 2: One product owner, multiple backlogs

In this strategy, the product owner maintains *multiple* product backlogs, one per team. We haven't actually tried this approach, but we've been close. This is basically our fallback plan in case the first approach fails.

The weakness of this strategy is that the product owner is allocating stories to teams, a task that teams probably are better at doing themselves.

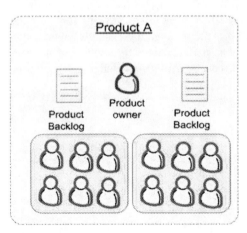

Strategy 3: Multiple product owners,
one backlog per owner

This is like the second strategy, one product backlog per team, but with one *product owner* per team as well!

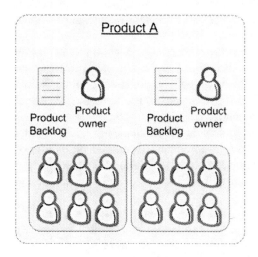

We haven't done this, and we probably never will.

If the two product backlogs involve the same code base, this will probably cause serious conflicts of interest between the two product owners.

If the two product backlogs involve separate codebases, this is essentially the same as splitting the whole product into separate sub-products and running them independently. This means we are back to the one-team-per-product situation, which is nice and easy.

Code branching

With multiple teams working on the same code base we inevitably have to deal with code branches in the SCM (software configuration management) system. There are lots of books and articles on how to deal with multiple people working on the same code base so I won't get into detail here. I don't have anything new or revolutionary to add. I will, however, summarize some of the most important lessons learned so far by our teams.

- Be strict about keeping the mainline (or trunk) in a consistent state. This means, at the very least, that everything should compile and all unit tests should pass. It should be possible to create a working release at *any given moment*. Preferably the continuous build system should build and auto-deploy to a test environment every night.

- Tag each release. Whenever you release to acceptance test or to production, make sure there is a version tag on your mainline identifying exactly what was released. That means you can, at any time in the future, go back and create a maintenance branch from that point.
- Create new branches only when necessary. A good rule of thumb is to branch off a new codeline *only* when you can't use an existing codeline without breaking that codeline's policy. When in doubt, don't branch. Why? Because each active branch costs in administration and complexity.
- Use branches primarily to separate *different lifecycles*. You may or may not decide to have each Scrum team code on their own codeline. But if you mix short-term fixes with long term changes on the same codeline, you will find it very difficult to release the short-term fixes!
- Synchronize often. If you are working on a branch, synchronize to mainline whenever you have something that builds. Every day when you get to work, synchronize from mainline to your branch, so that your branch is up-to-date with respect to other teams' changes. If this gives you merge-hell just accept the fact that it would have been even worse to wait.

Multi-team retrospectives

How do we do sprint retrospectives when there are multiple teams working on the same product?

Immediately after the sprint demo, after the applause and the mingle, each team goes off to a room of their own, or to some comfortable out-of-office location. They do their retrospectives pretty much as I described on pg 67 "How we do Sprint retrospectives".

During the sprint planning meeting (which all teams attend, since we do synchronized sprints within each product), the first thing we do is let one spokesman from each team stand up and summarize the key points from their retrospective. Takes about 5 minutes per team. Then we have open discussion for about 10 – 20 minutes. Then we take a break. Then we start the actual sprint planning.

We haven't tried any other way for multiple teams, this works good enough. The biggest disadvantage is that there is no slack time after the sprint retrospective part, before the sprint planning part of the meeting. (See pg 73 "Slack time between sprints")

For single-team products, we don't do any retrospective summary during the sprint planning meeting. No need to, since everybody was present at the actual retrospective meeting.

16

How we handle geographically distributed teams

What happens when team members are in different geographic locations? Much of the Scrum and XP "magic" is based on co-located tightly collaborating team members that pair program and meet face-to-face every day.

We have some geographically separated teams, and we also have team members working from home from time to time.

Our strategy for this is quite simple. We use every trick we can come up with to maximize the communication bandwidth between the physically separated team members. I don't only mean communication bandwidth as in Mbit/second (although that is of course important as well). I mean communication bandwidth in a wider sense:

- The ability to pair program together.
- The ability to meet face-to-face at the daily scrum.
- The ability to have face-to-face discussions at any time.
- The ability to meet physically and socialize.
- The ability to have spontaneous meetings with the whole team.
- The ability to see the same view of the sprint backlog, sprint burndown, product backlog, and other information radiators.

Some of the measures we have implemented (or are implementing, we haven't done them all yet) are:
- Webcam and headset at each workstation.
- "Remote-enabled" conference rooms with webcams, conference microphones, always-on-always-ready computers, desktop sharing software, etc.
- "Remote windows". Big screens at each location, showing a permanent view of the other locations. Sort of like a virtual window between two departments. You can stand there and

wave. You can see who is at his desk and who is talking to who. This is to create a feeling of "hey we're in this together".

- Exchange programs, where people from each location travel and visit each other on a regular basis.

Using these techniques and more we are slowly but surely starting to get the hang of how to do sprint planning meetings, demos, retrospectives, daily scrums, etc, with team members distributed geographically.

As usual it's all about experimenting. Inspect => adapt => inspect => adapt => inspect => adapt => inspect => adapt => inspect => adapt

Offshoring

We have several offshore teams and have been experimenting with how to handle this efficiently using Scrum.

There are two main strategies here: separated teams or separated team members.

Separated teams

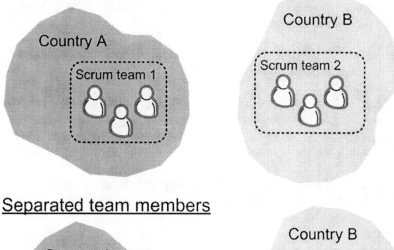

Separated team members

The first strategy, separated teams, is a compelling choice. Nevertheless, we have started with the second strategy, separated team members. There are several reasons for this.

1. We want the team members to get to know each other well.
2. We want excellent communication infrastructure between the two locations, and want to give the teams a strong incentive to set this up.
3. In the beginning, the offshore team is too small to form an effective scrum team on their own.
4. We want a period of intense knowledge sharing before independent offshore teams will be a feasible option.

In the long run we may well move towards the "separated teams" strategy.

Team members working from home

Working from home can be really good sometimes. Sometimes you can get more programming done in one day at home than a whole week at work. At least if you don't have kids :o)

Yet one of the fundamentals in Scrum is that the whole team should be physically collocated. So what do we do?

Basically we leave it to the teams to decide when and how often it is OK to work from home. Some team members work from home regularly due to long commutes. We do, however, encourage the teams to be physically collocated "most" of the time.

When team members work from home they join the daily scrum using a Skype voice call (sometimes video). They are online through instant messaging all day. Not as good as being in the same room, but good enough.

We once tried the concept of having Wednesdays designated as *focus day*. That basically meant "if you would like to work from home, that's fine, but do it on Wednesdays. And check with your team" This worked pretty well with the team that we tried it on. Usually most of the team stayed home on Wednesdays and they get a lot done, while still collaborating fairly well. Since it only was one day, the team members didn't get too out-of-sync with each other. For some reason this never quite caught on with the other teams though.

On the whole people working from home has not really been a problem for us.

17

Scrum master checklist

In this final chapter I will show you our scrum master "checklist", listing the most common administrative routines of our Scrum masters. Stuff that is easy to forget. We skip the obvious things such as "remove impediments from the team".

Beginning of sprint

- After the Sprint planning meeting, create a Sprint info page.
    - o Add a link to your page from the dashboard on the wiki.
    - o Print the page and put it on the wall where people pass by your team.
- Send an email to everyone announcing that a new sprint is started. Include the sprint goal and a link to the Sprint info page.
- Update the sprint statistics document. Add your estimated velocity, team size, sprint length, etc.

Every day

- Make sure the Daily Scrum meeting is started and ended on time.
- Make sure Stories are added/removed from the Sprint backlog as necessary to keep the sprint on schedule.
    - o Make sure the Product owner is notified of these changes.
- Make sure the Sprint backlog and burndown is kept up-to-date by the team.
- Make sure problems/impediments are solved or reported to Product owner and/or Chief of development.

End of sprint

- Do an open Sprint demo.
- Everyone should be notified about the demo a day or two before.
- Do a Sprint retrospective with the whole team and Product owner. Invite Chief of development as well, so he can help spread the lessons learned.
- Update the sprint statistics document. Add the actual velocity and key points from the retrospective.

18

Parting words

Whew! Never thought it would get this long.

Hope this paper gave you some useful ideas, whether you are new to Scrum or a seasoned veteran.

Since Scrum must be tailored specifically to each environment it is hard to argue constructively over best practices at a general level. Nevertheless I'm interested in hearing your feedback. Tell me how your approach differs from mine. Give me ideas on how to improve!

Feel free to contact me at **henrik.kniberg@crisp.se**.
I also keep an eye on **scrumdevelopment@yahoogroups.com**.

If you liked this book you might want to check in on my blog from time to time. I hope to be adding some posts on Java and agile software development.
http://blog.crisp.se/henrikkniberg/

Oh, and don't forget...

It's just a job right?

Recommended reading

Here are some books that have provided me with lots of inspiration and ideas. Highly recommended!

About the author

Henrik Kniberg (henrik.kniberg@crisp.se) is a consultant at Crisp in Stockholm (www.crisp.se), specializing in Java and Agile software development.

Ever since the first XP books and the agile manifesto appeared Henrik has embraced agile principals and tried to learn how to apply them efficiently in different types of organizations. As co-founder and CTO of Goyada 1998-2003 he had ample opportunity to experiment with test-driven development and other agile practices as a he built and managed a technical platform and a 30-person development team.

In late 2005 Henrik was contracted as chief of development at a Swedish company in the gaming business. The company was in a crisis situation with urgent organizational and technical problems. Using Scrum and XP as a tool, Henrik helped the company out of the crisis by implementing agile and lean principles at all levels in the company.

One Friday in November 2006 Henrik was home in bed with a fever and decided to jot down some notes for himself about what he had learned over the past year. Once he started writing, however, he couldn't stop and after three days of frantic typing and drawing, the initial notes had grown into an 80-page article entitled "Scrum and XP from the Trenches", which ultimately became this book.

Henrik takes a holistic approach and enjoys adopting different roles such as manager, developer, scrummaster, teacher, and coach. He is passionate about helping companies build excellent software and excellent teams, taking on whatever role is necessary.

Henrik grew up in Tokyo and now lives in Stockholm with his wife Sophia and two kids. He is an active musician on his freetime, composing music and playing bass and keyboard with local bands.
For more info see http://www.crisp.se/henrik.kniberg

Printed in the United States
105943LV00003B/391-396/A

9 781430 322641